THE
LUNAR
Sabbath
CONSPIRACY

by Terri Heagy

GATE Publishing

Editing by Helen Heavirland
Editorial assistance by Gary Heagy
Book cover and interior design by Emily Heagy

All Scripture quotations are from the New King James Version unless otherwise noted.

All emphasis and words in brackets within quotations are added by the author.

ISBN: 978-0-615-39581-4

Contents

A FRIEND

I knew I had found a friend when she came into my life. At the time we both had small children we were starting to homeschool. We shared ideas and dreams as only young mothers could. Though she displayed quiet control, she was full of energy and creativeness. Who else would think of roasting mini-marshmallows over a flaming candle as entertainment? We would join our children in this giggling fun.

When I went through a hard time in my life, she prayed with me regularly and shared spiritually uplifting passages. Her life, though plagued by her own personal challenges, revealed only spiritual sweetness. This was the Laura Lee Vornholt-Jones I knew.

Giving up "pagan" holidays caused her to look for ways to fill the gap for her five growing children. I suppose this may have been the reason they chose to observe the feast days as did the ancient Jews. This meant following a traditional Jewish calendar. Since the Hebrew feasts are tied to the lunar calendar, this eventually led her to connecting the weekly Sabbath to the moon as well.

Laura Lee and I have had many conversations about her new beliefs. She and her mother, eLaine Vornholt, wrote the books *The Great Calendar Controversy, History of a Lie,* and most recently *Calendar Fraud!* They developed a website to promote the Lunar Sabbath, which is spreading around the world. They still claim to be strong believers of the Seventh-day Adventist doctrines and emphatically proclaim belief in the writings of Ellen G. White.

Laura Lee challenged me to study the Lunar Sabbath and the change of the calendars through history to see if what I believed as a Saturday Sabbath-keeper was really true. Is Saturday truly the Sabbath? I was willing to give up my preconceived ideas for new light, if the truth bore witness to a different way than I had been taught.

This book is the result of my searching. I am not a theologian, historian, or philosopher—just a layperson using sources available to anybody. I do not mean to attack Laura Lee or her mother (referred to in this book as the "Vornholts"). My only desire is to share in a loving way what I believe to be truth.

So why am I willing to put these theories openly to the test? Laura Lee told me that she felt the writing of her books would be worth it if it caused people to study deeper, no matter what conclusion they came to. I pray that my study can help others understand the Lunar Sabbath theory better so with the guidance of the Holy Spirit, they may find and choose to follow God's true Sabbath.

Terri Heagy

SOME DEFINITIONS

Lunar Sabbath – A theory that uses the moon to determine the days the sanctified Sabbaths fall on, rather than a continuous seven-day weekly cycle.

Luni-solar Calendar – The calendar based on the moon and sun used by several ancient nations (particularly the Jews) for the observation of their yearly religious feasts.

Lunar Sabbatarians – People who observe the Sabbath with the Luni-solar calendar method.

Sabbath – To "cease" or "rest." Sabbath can refer to ceremonial days in which the Jews were to cease from their work, or it can refer to the sanctified Sabbath of the Lord God which is observed every seven days. Sometimes "sabbaths" can mean weeks or "sevens."

Seventh-day Sabbath – Used to define the Sabbath as kept by Seventh-day Adventists and Jews on the day known as Saturday.

Week – Literally "seven" and is in reference to a continuous seven-day weekly cycle that is not connected to any natural phenomenon.

CHAPTER 1

LUNAR LIGHT

THE SABBATH

Of all the world's holy days, holidays, and festivals, the Sabbath exists as the oldest. God sanctified it during the creation week almost 6,000 years ago. Many people don't recognize it for its value and either ignore it or rely instead on traditions from hundreds of years past. The Sabbath has been trampled and abused for generations, even by people who knew about it. But does it still have the same importance as it did in the beginning? Orthodox Jews and Sabbath-keeping Christians such as Seventh-day Adventists believe it does.

These faithful Sabbath-keepers look back at Creation as the source for this holy day. God created a beautiful world in six days and paused the seventh day to admire, with His human beings, the new home He had created.

God sanctified the seventh day for mankind. Humans can lay aside their labor and have a guilt-free day to enjoy life with God. By taking our eyes off our own interests and pursuits for one day to contemplate God's love for us in praise and thanksgiving, we may gain strength and victory over Satan's snares.

God states that the Sabbath is a sign between Him and His people. "Therefore the children of Israel shall keep the Sabbath, to observe the Sabbath throughout their generations as a perpetual covenant. It is a sign between Me and the children of Israel forever; for in six days the LORD made the heavens and the earth, and on the seventh day He rested and was refreshed."[1]

"Since the Lord inaugurated the Sabbath before nationalities or races existed, it is truly universal. God intended it for all men everywhere. Whoever we are and wherever we are, the Lord wants us to be His guest in a special way on the Sabbath."[2]

God designed the seventh day as a test of who His people were throughout the history of this earth.[3] Revelation states that in the end of time God's people, having His seal rather than the mark of the beast, are those who still keep His commandments, including the Sabbath (those who worship Him who made heaven and earth and sea!).[4] It seems the Sabbath is a serious covenant with God.

SATAN ATTACKS THE TRUE SABBATH

Since the fall of man, Satan has tried to take man's eyes from God and claim the earth as his own. He has no love for mankind. He only uses them to elevate himself to be as

God. He envies God's position without any sense for the pure and lovely character that imparts peace and joy for all. He only wants the honor and power God has.

One of the best ways Satan has found to separate man from his Creator is to erode the time they spend together. Not only on a daily basis does Satan attempt to separate God and man, but especially on the hallowed Sabbath God designed for close communion. Since God sanctified the Sabbath day and made it a sign between Him and His people, that day has become a specific target of the enemy.

"Satan has worked through deception to institute a spurious Sabbath, that the worship of God's people might become an offense to the Creator."[5] Knowing the faithful observance of Sabbath would keep human beings from turning away from God, Satan strove to get man to change the emphasis of the holy Sabbath to a different day.

If keeping the correct Sabbath is important to God, and we know Satan is trying to deceive people away from the true Sabbath, how do we know for certain that we are keeping the correct day holy?

Seventh-day Adventists believe that Saturday is God's Holy Sabbath. There has long been an outside pressure that Sunday has become the Sabbath due to Christ's resurrection making that the Lord's Day. However, now there is an attack on the Saturday Sabbath coming from inside the church in the form of the Lunar Sabbath movement.

THE LUNAR SABBATH

According to Lunar Sabbath authors eLaine Vornholt and Laura Lee Vornholt-Jones, neither Sunday nor Saturday Sabbath-keepers keep the correct Biblical day. Jews and Seventh-day Adventists keep a continuous weekly cycle with every seventh day for the Sabbath. According to our calendar that seventh day lands on Saturday. But the Vornholts argue that this day and the weekly cycle refer to pagan worship just as much as the day Sunday.

They feel the solution rests in the Jewish luni-solar calculation of the feasts God implemented for the children of Israel. God gave instructions that the new moon day (the first sign of the new crescent) would start the count of days to certain seasonal feasts. Lunar Sabbatarians believe that the weekly Sabbath should be calculated in the same way as those feasts—using the new moon each month to define that month's Sabbath days.

According to those who follow the Lunar Sabbath idea, the new moon day is the first Sabbath of a month, no matter what day of our civil calendar falls on. Seven days later (the 8th day from the new moon) is the next Sabbath. The 15th, 22nd and 29th days from the new moon are also Sabbaths. They say no one can ever doubt when the true Sabbath falls because we have had the moon since Creation and it can perpetually show us the truth. Every month this calculation begins again is based on the new moon. This is what is referred to as "Lunar Sabbaths."

Are Sabbath-keepers being deceived by Satan into

observing a false Sabbath? Could it be true that the current calendar which shows Saturday as the seventh day of the week is in error? Is God's Sabbath truly determined by the cycle of the moon?

NEW LIGHT?

When I first heard about the Lunar Sabbath concept I was shocked. Was I missing something? This idea sounded different, but intriguing to me. The Vornholts claimed the theory was "new light." They used this quote (and many more like it) to claim that the Lunar Sabbath is new light which we must follow:

> Those who cling to old customs and hoary errors have lost sight of the fact that light is ever increasing upon the path of all who follow Christ; truth is constantly unfolding to the people of God. We must be continually advancing if we are following our Leader. . . . We cannot be excusable in accepting only the light which our fathers had one hundred years ago. If our God-fearing fathers had seen what we see, and heard what we hear, they would have accepted the light, and walked in it. If we desire to imitate their faithfulness, we must receive the truths open to us, as they received those presented to them; we must do as they would have done, had they lived in our day.[6]

I am not opposed to new light. As a Seventh-day Adventist, I found the subject interesting because of the Vornholts' use of both Scripture and Spirit of Prophecy (traditional Seventh-day Adventists and the Vornholts agree that Spirit of Prophecy includes the writings of Ellen

G. White). If the Lunar Sabbath theory really could stand in harmony with the inspired writings, the truth would come out clearly and I would follow it.

I had known the Jewish people used a luni-solar calendar to determine their spiritual feasts (some days were even called sabbaths) so I wondered if this really could apply to the seventh-day Sabbath as well.

I started out by studying what the Bible and Spirit of Prophecy[7] said about the Sabbath truth. "To the law and to the testimony! If they do not speak according to this word, it is because there is no light in them."[8]

I then checked out stacks of books regarding the Sabbath from my church library and other libraries and ordered books I couldn't obtain locally. I spent hours sifting through information on the internet. I spoke to a number of people I felt were Bible scholars, asking various questions. My favorite tools were the Power Bible program and my Ellen White software containing all her writings.[9] I found them to be so valuable I joked to my husband that if I ever had to flee to the mountains to escape persecution for my faith, my laptop would come with me!

With all the information I found, I believed I had a solid understanding of the biblical Sabbath, the history of the calendar, and feast days. Only then did I start a more thorough study of the Vornholts' theories on their website[10] and in their books.

Some points of the Lunar Sabbath theory made sense, others seemed like speculation. But when I saw their chart of a lunar month and how the Sabbath was laid out through the phases of the moon, I found myself suddenly very confused. I had never thought about how the phases of the moon worked before. When the moon became dark at the end of the lunar month did it take a long time (another week?) to be seen again? I was trying to fit the Lunar Sabbaths into my continuous weekly cycle concept. What I didn't realize at the time was that the Lunar Sabbatarians didn't believe in a continuous weekly cycle.

I was glad my husband was also studying the topic and we could discuss our questions and conclusions (some of the research in this book is from his study). I had an impression to fit two lunar month charts together side by side, but didn't understand enough to know how. My husband came to my rescue and made a chart (see following page) so I could see how the lunar month cycle worked from month to month. Suddenly, my mind cleared and I saw the lunar weeks float through our civil calendar. One month their Sabbath could fall on a Tuesday and the next, a different day.

NON-DAYS?

Because the lunar month is only 29 and sometimes 30 days long, it is impossible for more than four complete weeks to fit into the moon's phases without extra days left over. So the "week" resets again at the next new moon. This causes two "Sabbaths" to be celebrated side-by-side at the end of the month. The Vornholts call this a "long weekend," a concept not mentioned anywhere in the Bible or Spirit of Prophecy.

When some months have a 30th day, what do you do with that extra day? The Lunar Sabbatarians method of dealing with these extra days is to call them "non-days." A "non-day"?

The problem with the "non-day" concept is that the Bible clearly defines a day as an evening and a morning.[11] Using logic and reversing this formula, if you have an evening and a morning, you must have a day. So how can you call a 24-hour period that has an evening and morning a "non-day" as if it doesn't exist or doesn't count for anything? Can you ignore that the day has occurred?

LUNAR WEEKS COMPARED TO THE COMMON CALENDAR

S	M	T	W	Th	F	Sa
24	25	26	27	28	29	1
2	3	4	5	6	7	8
9	10	11	12	13	14	15
16	17	18	19	20	21	22
23	24	25	26	27	28	29
1	2	3	4	5	6	7
8	9	10	11	12	13	14
15	16	17	18	19	20	21
22	23	24	25	26	27	28
29	*	1	2	3	4	5
6	7	8	9	10	11	12
13	14	15	16	17	18	19
20	21	22	23	24	25	26
27	28	29	1	2	3	4
5	6	7	8	9	10	11

Numbers in dark boxes (all 1's) represent "New Moon" Sabbaths. Numbers in shading (all 8's, 15's, 22's, 29's) represent "seventh-day" Sabbaths
The asterisk represents a "non-day"

Things that exist cannot disappear just by saying that they don't exist. We can't say that we have non-children, non-cancer, non-body fat, non-sins, non-debts... There is no way that we can delete a day from our calendar by just calling it a "non-day."

How would you function on a "non-day?" It is not a Sabbath. It is not a working day. The Bible gives no clue as to how to observe one—which is a bit suspicious. If God designed our lives to function with something as critical as "non-days," which go along with correct Sabbath-keeping, He would have told us about it in His Word. But the Bible makes not even the slightest mention of a "non-day" or a "long weekend."

When I saw this, God opened my eyes. Lunar Sabbatarians resetting their week at every new moon and having extra days not accounted for were my first clues that the Lunar Sabbath theory had some serious errors. The Bible plainly teaches that God made the week with every seventh day as the Sabbath. Nowhere in the scriptures or writings of Ellen White does it say anything about two Sabbaths being observed together, skipping a "non-day" or even resetting the weekly cycle with the new moon. God commanded us to keep every seventh day holy, not the 8th, or the 15th, or the 22nd, or the 29th.

THE LUNAR SABBATH COMMANDMENT

There is no commandment anywhere in the scriptures which says:

> On the day following the new moon of each month, six days shall work be done, but the seventh day is the Sabbath of Yahweh your Elohim. You shall do this for four weeks. Then, depending on whether the new month has started, you shall not engage in commerce or paid work for 1 or 2 days. Then you shall reset your week into the "Six days shall work be done, but the seventh day is a Sabbath of solemn rest" pattern.[12]

"The lack of such a command is damaging to the Lunar Sabbath theory. If God did not specifically define a seventh-day Sabbath other than on a weekly cycle, then something is being added to His express command. Adding to His commandments is breaking His law."[13] This is serious.

God never said any such thing, but this is the commandment that Lunar Sabbatarians follow. We must be careful when we try to do things our own way. God said, "Whatever I command you, be careful to observe it; *you shall not add to it nor take away from it.*"[14]

> If we take the scriptures for what they say, not adding anything to it, we can only arrive at an understanding that God's Sabbath falls on an uninterruptable seven-day (weekly) rotation. There really isn't room for any other possible interpretations. Six days you labor, and you rest on the seventh.[15]

Praise the Lord for giving us His Word as a safeguard

from all deception. We need to put our trust in Him and take Him at His Word, and He will guide us to the truth.

---

1. Exodus 31:16–17.
2. Kubo, Sakae. *God Meets Man* (Tennessee: Southern Publishing Association, 1978), p. 19.
3. Exodus 31:13.
4. Revelation 7:3, 14:7, 14:12, 12:17, 14:7, Exodus 20:11.
5. White, Ellen G. *Review and Herald,* September 13, 1898, par. 2.
6. White, Ellen G. *Historical Sketches,* p. 197.
7. The terms "Spirit of Prophecy" and "Ellen White" are used interchangeably.
8. Isaiah 8:20.
9. Ellen White stands as the most prolific writer of America and the most prolific female writer of the world. The software indexes her writings for easy searching.
10. See 4angelspublications.com.
11. Genesis 1:5.
12. Eliyah, "Beware of the Lunar Sabbath," see eliyah.com.
13. Ibid.
14. Deuteronomy 12:32, emphasis supplied.
15. Eliyah, op. cit.

CHAPTER 2

WHEN *IS* THE LUNAR SABBATH?

CONFUSING THEORIES

As I began to study the Lunar Sabbath theory to determine if it was true, there were a number of red flags that jumped out at me. The "non-days" I just mentioned was the first. In researching on the internet I quickly came to the realization that there are various theories regarding the Lunar Sabbath. I was struck by the confusion, differing opinions, and complexity of the various theories. How could a person know for certain how and when to keep it, since the Bible and Spirit of Prophecy give no explanation about the Lunar Sabbath?

Many Lunar Sabbath websites claim to have all the truth and they spend their efforts disputing with other Lunar Sabbath theories—when a day begins, sunrise or sunset theories, how and when to keep which days, whether to make non-days or long weekends holy or not, how to start counting from the new moon, and many other topics. The whole thing is a mass of confusion.

I apologize if some of my facts in this book about what Lunar Sabbatarians believe do not seem accurate to other Lunar Sabbath groups. Because the theories are so diverse, it is hard to nail down one specific set of beliefs that apply to every version of the theory. Most of the Lunar Sabbatarian concepts I discuss in this book come from the Vornholts' books *The Great Calendar Controversy* and *History of a Lie* because these publications pertain mainly to the beliefs of Seventh-day Adventists.

THE CORRECT DAY FOR A LUNAR SABBATH

Among the various Lunar Sabbatarians, there is confusion on exactly how to determine the start of a new lunar month. If you don't know exactly when the month starts, then during that month your Sabbaths might be off and you could be keeping the wrong day.

Some Lunar Sabbatarians count the seven days so the sabbaths fall on the 7th, 14th, 21st and 28th days. Others are just one day off, marking their sabbaths on the 8th, 15th, 22nd and 29th days. These systems ignore God's command to just keep every seventh day holy.[1]

How do you know who is right? There is no biblical evidence to prove any of the theories without a doubt. An associate of the Vornholts in promoting the Lunar Sabbath, who also comes from a Seventh-day Adventist background, has written the following statement in one of her articles:

When I first discovered Holy Appointed Festivals and the corresponding luni-solar truth, I found it disconcerting that there could be so many claims as to when the New Moon actually occurred. I also realized that this would continue to be the case as long as we are on earth and Satan has the freedoms he has to deceive....

In the beginning of my luni-solar journey I began by observing the first visible crescent New Moon, and did so for several months. Then after reading some other websites I switched and began to follow the dark conjunction phase for a short period of time....

... I have come full circle back to observing the first visible crescent moon as Yahweh's New Moon beacon in the heavens. If I am yet incorrect on my decision to observe the first visible crescent New Moon, I believe Yahweh will lead me.[2]

This lady promotes the Lunar Sabbath theory worldwide via articles and websites. She has gone through a struggle over how to keep the correct Sabbath and is still not 100% positive about her decision as to which day to observe. Keeping the wrong day for Sabbath is a serious offense according to God. How will she know when she is absolutely sure she is doing it right? If she does figure it out so she is totally confident that she is right, how will she convince all the other Lunar Sabbatarians of the "truth?"

BIBLICAL OBSERVATION

God originally designed for the Jewish people to chart their feast days by the sighting of the new moon.[3] Observers would be just outside of Jerusalem anticipating the first light of the crescent moon. As soon as they would see it they would hurry to the Sanhedrin in Jerusalem (the Hebrew's highest court) and state their observation. The men were carefully questioned and if two men were counted as witnesses, then the Sanhedrin made their announcement the next morning. The new month had started and they could start counting to the next feast.

There were challenges to this method. Sometimes the sky may have been cloudy or the moon was not visible. If no one witnessed the new moon, then the new month was delayed a day and all the dates of the coming month were thus set. It wasn't that the Sanhedrin didn't know when the moon was scheduled to appear, but rather that the sanctification of the moon had to be made according to eyewitness reports.[4]

There were more factors besides the sighting of a new moon to start their religious new year. The barley harvest had to be ready and if it wasn't, the Jews delayed the Passover feast another month. Again, this was only done by observation.

Once the new month was confirmed in Jerusalem, and if it was a month of a feast, an announcement was relayed throughout the land (up to 14 days away) of the start of the month. Obviously, the announcement could not be made until the next morning. This meant that Jews not living near Jerusalem couldn't observe new moon days because they wouldn't have the announcement of the official new moon sighting until after it happened.

Because of the slowness of communication many didn't

learn of the sighting until around the time for the feast to start, 14 days later. Historically, if the Jews didn't get an announcement in time, they would observe two days for the feast just to make sure they got the right day.

This brings up an important and obvious question. If they were keeping the Sabbath through the same luni-solar system as the Lunar Sabbatarians claim, then how would the poor Jews living outside of Jerusalem ever know when the correct Sabbath day was meant to be? Would they keep two Sabbath days together every week? That would break the commandment to work six days before resting on the following Sabbath. Or if they kept the Sabbath day based on their own observations, when official word arrived, they might be keeping the Sabbath on the wrong day, thus breaking the commandment! If they were breaking the Sabbath commandment, they were worthy of death. But would that be fair if they didn't know when the new moon was officially observed in Jerusalem?

That problem is still relevant today, if we are to keep the luni-solar calendar by the observation of the new moon. M. L. Andreason, of the 1938 Seventh-day Adventist Research Committee, questioned how someone could determine the precise new moon day in North America for religious reasons, when God ordained it from Jerusalem.

> Definite problems occur, however, when attempts are made to apply to the world that which was designed for a small, compact country. These problems are greatly magnified when determination of New Year and feast days is based upon local observations and computations. According to this plan each

community decides for itself when the phasis [sic] of the moon occur, and adjusts its New Year and feasts accordingly. It thus becomes not only possible, but inevitable, that a community located some distance west of the preceding lunar day line would, should the new lunar day line fall between it and the former line, observe the coming feasts a day earlier than the community located east of the line.[5]

The sighting of the new moon in biblical times was always determined by observation from Jerusalem, rather than using calculation. However, the Lunar Sabbatarian believers currently use man-made calculations rather than the "observation reckoning" God originally designed for determining feasts.

It seems safe to say that keeping the Lunar Sabbath correctly can be very tricky and confusing. And if it is so difficult to keep the exact day according to biblical standards, would God be fair to judge us without giving specific instructions to this Lunar Sabbath problem?

SIMPLICITY VS. COMPLEXITY

God made the Sabbath at Creation to be easily understood. Six days you work and the seventh is the Sabbath. M. L. Andreason noted, "The seventh-day Sabbath is clear and distinct. A child can understand its computation."[6]

With the Lunar Sabbath theory, you almost need to get a college degree to understand all of the issues, calendation principles, etc. Just try to read some of their explanations about how to figure it all out! Here is a small example of the process used to determine which day of the month the Sabbath begins:

> *Question:* Does the "dark conjunction" lunar phase receive more light than the previous night, as in the waxing phases or less light than the previous day, as in the waning phases?
>
> *Answer:* It displays less light as in the waning phases. The reason this is so important to understand is that because the "dark conjunction phase" has all the markings of a waning phase, it is therefore self-evident that it belongs to the end of the second half of the old month. Neither can it be both part of the old month and part of the beginning of a new month. Since it appears to be in the waning category it cannot be a "new" refreshed moon beginning a new month. This darkest phase of the month is forever grouped with the waning phases as they, day by day, receive less and less light of the sun until it is completely void of light. Therefore by definition the dark "conjunction phase" is a waning phase and always part of the second half of the old lunar month. Never can it be any portion of the waxing phases of a "new" month, as these alone are receiving more and more light with each phase than the preceding phase until the moon is full.[7]

Does this help you understand better when to keep the Sabbath? Yet this is only a taste of the complexity and confusion that exists in understanding the Lunar Sabbath system.

Our God is not a god of confusion. He does not make His commands so complicated that most people are confounded by them, especially when it comes to the special time He has set aside to meet with us.

1. Eliyah, "Beware of the Lunar Sabbath," see eliyah.com.

2. French, Kerrie. "The New Moon, When Is It?" (E-mail article)

3. Deuteronomy 16:1.

4. "The New Moon and the Power of Judaism," see beingjewish.com.

5. Undated letter from M. L. Andreason to Grace Amadon, p. 1.

6. Ibid, p. 6.

7. French, op. cit.

CHAPTER 3

MOONS, FEASTS, AND SABBATHS

SABBATHS AND FEASTS

The Jews had several feasts that occurred throughout the year celebrating various seasons. Their year began with the Passover month in the spring, just before their barley ripened. In Leviticus 23, Moses describes these feasts as special days to be kept every year. However, before these feasts are detailed, the Sabbath is mentioned.

> And the LORD spoke to Moses, saying, "Speak to the children of Israel, and say to them: 'The feasts of the LORD, which you shall proclaim to be holy convocations, these are My feasts. Six days shall work be done, but the seventh day is a Sabbath of solemn rest, a holy convocation. You shall do no work on it; it is the Sabbath of the LORD in all your dwellings. These are the feasts of the LORD, holy convocations which you shall proclaim at their appointed times. . . .'"[1]

This is the scripture which leads Lunar Sabbatarians into thinking the seventh-day Sabbath is linked with the Jewish feast days. It is actually the cornerstone text of their whole theory. They state the Sabbath heads the list as the very first feast day mentioned. From this they conclude that the luni-solar calendar is used to calculate the weekly Sabbath as well as the feasts.

Seventh-day Adventists do not agree that Leviticus 23 shows the Sabbath as one of the general feast days. A good interpretation of these verses, showing the Seventh-day Adventist view, is from *The Clear Word* paraphrase by Jack Blanco.

> Then the Lord said to Moses, "Speak to the children of Israel and tell them about the appointed feasts. They are to be regarded as sacred festivals of worship set apart by Me. There has always been the weekly Sabbath. Six days are set aside for your regular work, but the seventh day is the Sabbath, a day of solemn rest. On that day all work must stop because it is the day the Lord has set aside for worship. The day belongs to me no matter where the children of Israel live. *In addition to the weekly Sabbath,* there are six sacred assemblies to be kept every year which are special for all. Three of these are religious festivals."[2]

MO'ED

An argument made to tie the seventh-day Sabbath to the feast days involves the use of the word *mo'ed.* It is found in the creation account as well as in the description of the feasts in Leviticus. In seeing *mo'ed* in Genesis 1, Lunar Sabbatarians claim that this proves the Lunar Sabbath originated at Creation.

After creating the lights in the firmament, God designated

them for signs, seasons (the Hebrew word *mo'ed* meaning a yearly festival, convocation, or feast), days and years.

> And God said, Let there be lights in the firmament of the heaven to divide the day from the night; and let them be for signs, and for seasons [*mo'ed*], and for days, and years.[3]

Notice that God said the lights were to help distinguish seasons, days and years—not weeks. God uses the week as a witness of His creative power because it is not connected with anything in nature. God identified His Sabbath day as the day following the six days during which He created. He commanded His people to rest every seventh day in honor of this magnificent accomplishment.

However, Lunar Sabbatarians take the verse from the creation week about the moon being created for seasons *(mo'ed)* and show that in Leviticus 23 every time the word "feasts" comes up it is the same word. They say the Sabbath is part of the *mo'ed* because all of God's worship days in the Bible are called a *mo'ed*. But the sanctified Sabbath in these verses is never classified as a *mo'ed* (remember this word signals a "*yearly* feast").

> And the Lord spoke to Moses, saying, "Speak to the children of Israel, and say to them: The *Feasts* [*mo'ed*] of the Lord, which you shall proclaim to be holy convocations, these are My *feasts* [*mo'ed*]. Six days shall work be done, but the seventh day is a Sabbath of solemn rest, a holy convocation. You shall do no work on it; it is the Sabbath of the Lord in all your dwellings."[4]

The Sabbath is not considered one of the yearly feasts, but rather a day that is observed in addition to the feast days. This is made even more clear in Leviticus 23:38. After describing all the offerings and sacrifices to be made on the feast days, Scripture stops and states in verse 38, "—besides the Sabbaths of the Lord, besides your gifts, besides all your vows, besides all your freewill offerings which you give to the Lord."

The Hebrew word for "besides" [*bad*] means "separate" or "apart from." This verse suggests the Sabbath is something already in place, and it is apart from the newly appointed feasts.

Other places in Scripture repeat the list of yearly feasts from Leviticus 23, such as Deuteronomy 16 and Exodus 16:14-19. However, the Sabbath fails to be included with these lists. It obviously is a day of its own and not a *mo'ed*.

THE ORIGIN OF FEASTS

The original Sabbath of creation week was designed and given to perfect humans in a perfect world. Nothing blighted the beauty of the Garden of Eden or the perfection of Adam and Eve's characters. God communicated daily with them, and their happiness was supreme. Only when sin marred their characters and their land did God implement His plan of redemption through the institution of the sacrificial system.

Immediately after Adam and Eve left the garden they sacrificed a lamb in faith that God would save them from their sins. If sin had never occurred on this planet, there would have been no sacrificial system or feast days. There would have been no need for them.

It wasn't until twenty-five hundred years after Creation, when the Israelites escaped from slavery in Egypt, that God introduced to Moses the religious monthly cycle in reference to observing feast days, with the Passover month being the first of the year.[5]

What were the meanings of the feasts? Here are a few:

- *Passover*—Only the blood of Jesus Christ saves us from death.
- *Unleavened bread*—Christ alone is without sin.
- *First fruits*—Christ's victory gave a sample of the victory of the redeemed.
- *Tabernacles*—God saves us from slavery through Christ.
- *Day of Atonement*—Christ cleanses us from sin.

The sacrifices (and feast days) were specifically designed to point to the cross and also review how God had led Israel in the past through their struggles with evil.

Sabbath and the seven-day weekly cycle came out of a perfect, sinless world, celebrating the Creator and His power to create a perfect and beautiful earth in seven days. Conversely, the feasts came after sin entered the world and showed how God in His love and mercy saved us from the curse of sin.

THE "SABBATHS" VS.
THE SABBATH OF THE LORD

A few of the feast days were to be considered like a sabbath but not *the* seventh-day Sabbath. The confusion may come with the fact that the Bible mentions some of the feast days as sabbaths.

Study the following chart of comparisons[6] between the seventh-day Sabbath and ceremonial sabbaths and notice the differences.

	Seventh-day Sabbath	Ceremonial Sabbaths
1	Sanctified at Creation	Given at Sinai, 2500 years after Creation
2	Memorial of the beginning of time	Memorial of events in Jewish history
3	Intended to turn men back to Creation	Intended to point men forward to cross
4	God blessed and sanctified it	God did not bless, sanctify, or rest on them
5	Commemorates a perfect Creation	Commemorates events in a sinful world
6	Tied to the weekly cycle, always the same day of the week	Tied to the Jewish calendar, different day of the week each time celebrated
7	Kept anywhere in the world, because the weekly cycle operates free of all calendars	Known and kept only in the nation where the sacred calendar was in existence
8	Kept every week	Kept once a year
9	Made for all mankind	A part of that ceremonial ritual which was against us. Colossians 2:14
10	Will continue beyond this world	Abolished at Christ's crucifixion
11	No work in it	No servile work

We have holidays like Thanksgiving, when the family is home and spending time together. Many days are spent preparing food and planning activities for the special holiday. On the actual day we lay aside most of our work to spend together as a family and remember what we are thankful for. On many a holiday such as this, my children would say, "It felt like Sabbath today!" It was a special day, but that didn't make it *the* Sabbath.

The Jewish people celebrated the Sabbath with feasting and joy, but they knew the difference between it and the other feast days. Throughout the Bible there is a distinction between the feasts, new moons, and sabbaths of the Hebrews and the Sabbath of the Lord.

THE NEW MOON A SABBATH?

Because the new moons were so closely tied to the feast days, the new moon day also had a religious significance, although not considered a religious holy day. It was announced by trumpets as a celebration day, and everyone stopped work and holiday banquets were planned.[7] It was a totally separate type of festival, unlike the solemn feasts and the Sabbath day. New moon celebrations varied in degrees of holiness. This could be because a particular new moon was connected with looking forward to a special feast. It was ordained that it should be observed with certain specified offerings and rejoicing.[8]

Because additional sacrifices were offered on new moon days, the Vornholts consider new moon days more important than even the seventh-day Sabbath.

However, trying to prove from the Bible that the new

moon is a holy sabbath runs lunar theorists into serious problems. God specifically commanded that there was to be no work done on the Sabbath day. He actually had a man stoned to death for gathering wood for a fire on the Sabbath.[9]

Working on the Sabbath was obviously a serious offense. "But if you will not heed Me to hallow the Sabbath day, such as not carrying a burden when entering the gates of Jerusalem on the Sabbath day, then I will kindle a fire in its gates, and it shall devour the palaces of Jerusalem, and it shall not be quenched."[10]

But here are some scriptural instances where work or extensive travel happened on new moon days:

- Noah removed the covering of the ark on the first day of the moon.[11]

- On the first day of the second moon, a census was taken.[12]

- Ezra journeyed on two new moons.[13]

- The Israelites put up the tabernacle on the new moon at the command of God. This was a very labor-intense job.[14]

Because of the labor involved in these texts, the new moon could not be a holy Sabbath day. Either God is inconsistent by telling us it is all right to work on some Sabbaths and not on others, or one is the true Sabbath of Creation and the other is not.

God says He never changes. He is always the same.[15]

What a wonderful Friend to depend on!

1. Leviticus 23:1–4.

2. Blanco, Jack. *Clear Word Bible*, Leviticus 23:1–4 (Hagerstown, MD: Review & Herald, 1994), emphasis supplied.

3. Genesis 1:14.

4. Leviticus 23:1–3.

5. Exodus 12:2.

6. Tucker, J. L. *Another Look at the Christian Sabbath* (California: Quiet Hour Publication, 1977), p. 90–91, adapted.

7. "New Moon," *Smith's Bible Dictionary*, see biblestudytools.com.

8. "The New Moon and the Power of Judaism," see beingjewish.com.

9. Numbers 15:32–36.

10. Jeremiah 17:27.

11. Genesis 8:13.

12. Numbers 1:1.

13. Ezra 7:9.

14. Exodus 40:1, 2, 16, 17.

15. See Malachi 3:6; Hebrews 13:8.

CHAPTER 4

GOD PRESERVES A CONTINUOUS WEEK

THE TRUE WEEK OF CREATION

As mentioned in the previous chapter, Lunar Sabbatarians claim that the Lunar Sabbath was set in place at Creation and that the lunar cycle is the true "biblical week."

> But, lest after generations become confused and lose track of the days, God provided at Creation a built-in, ever present, always accurate clock/calendar to measure time and clearly designate the work days from the worship days. In order to worship God on the day He appointed, people must be able to understand how God's clock/calendar works *to know which day is number one,* the starting point for counting the six days to work, with worship on the seventh. The calendar God established at Creation was kept by the Jews until well into the 4th century AD. It was a luni-solar calendar with months lasting either 29 or 30 days.[1]

A critical question to ask is how to know what day number one is during the Creation week if you are to determine it by the moon. God created the moon on the fourth day, in the middle of the first week. The Bible describes the week as six evenings and mornings with the Sabbath ending it, so where would the Lunar Sabbath fit into that first week of Creation?

There is no way of knowing at what phase the moon was created. Even if it was a crescent moon when it was made (the fourth day of Creation), the Sabbath could not fall on day one or day eight of that very first lunar month. This is strikingly different than the seventh day of the week that God said He blessed.

The moon is not the foundation of the creation week. It is a lesser light to help define seasons. Other than claiming the *mo'ed* reference in Genesis 1:14 (as discussed in the previous chapter), Lunar Sabbatarians have no valid explanation as to how the Sabbath of creation is directed by the moon's cycles.

THE TRUE WEEK PRESERVED

Lunar Sabbatarians claim that there is no way that our weekly cycle could have possibly been preserved since Creation until the present time. Their book, *History of a Lie,* states, "It is understandable, though sad, that modern Christians assume the week as it is known today has cycled continuously and without interruption ever since Creation…"[2]

But can the God who created and sustained all things in the universe preserve something which is important to Him? Is He powerful enough to do that? If He was able to protect and preserve His Word until our modern times, isn't He powerful enough to preserve the weekly cycle to the end?

Inspiration clearly says that in fact God HAS preserved the weekly cycle of seven literal days since the time it was given to man until the present. "The *weekly cycle of seven literal days,* six for labor and the seventh for rest, *which has been preserved* and brought down through Bible history, originated in the great facts of the first seven days."[3]

Ellen White says she witnessed creation through visions of the Holy Spirit and gives a firsthand report of the creation week.

> I was then carried back to the creation, and was shown that the first week, in which God performed the work of creation in six days and rested on the seventh day, was *just like every other week.* The great God, in his days of creation and day of rest, *measured off the first cycle as a sample for successive weeks till the close of time.*[4]

Encyclopedia Britannica states, "the week is a period of seven days, having no reference whatever to the celestial motions—a circumstance to which it owes its unalterable uniformity... It has been employed from time immemorial in almost all eastern countries."[5]

EXPERT TESTIMONY OF THE CONTINUOUS WEEK

Seventh-day Adventist evangelist Mark Finley wrote to the Royal Greenwich Observatory in London, England concerning the continuity of the weekly cycle. The Observatory keeps an accurate record of time for the entire world. Their answer to his request was, "The continuity of the seven-day week has been maintained since the earliest days of the Jewish religion. The astronomer may be concerned in the decisions relating to the time, the calendar date, and the year number. But since the week is a civil, social and religious cycle, there is no reason why it should be disturbed by any adjustment of the calendar."[6]

James Robertson, Director American Ephemeris, Navy Department, U.S. Naval Observatory, Washington, D.C., March 12, 1932, said, "There has been no change in our calendar in past centuries that has affected in any way the cycle of the week."[7]

Dr. Frank Jeffries, Fellow of the Royal Astronomical Society and Research Director of the Royal Observatory, Greenwich, England stated, "It can be said with assurance that not a day has been lost since Creation, and all the calendar changes notwithstanding, there has been no break in the weekly cycle."[8]

THE WEEK NEVER LOST

The accusation is made by Lunar Sabbatarians that the seven-day weekly cycle as we know it did not survive since creation because the pagans messed with the days. "The pagan planetary week, like the Julian calendar that adopted it, is irreparably pagan."[9] They say that because pagans gave pagan names to the days of the week and made weeks of various numbers of days, we cannot trust the calendar we see before us. But just because the pagans fiddled with their calendars, does that automatically mean God's people lost the weekly cycle founded by God at the beginning?

Except for the interlude of the Hebrews almost losing the meaning of Sabbath sacredness during their Egyptian exile (but obviously restored during the exodus), it has been pointed out by numerous scholars that the weekly cycle has been observed carefully since Creation. However, we do not need to go back that far. When Jesus was on the earth, He observed the Sabbath. In doing so He, God Almighty, confirmed the correctness of whatever method was being used to determine the Sabbath during His time.

Our task, then, is to resolve whether Christ kept a Lunar Sabbath or the Sabbath of a continuous weekly cycle. The history since Christ can let us know if the method of His Sabbath keeping passed through time to our day.

HISTORY OF THE WEEKLY CYCLE PRIOR TO CHRIST

In the early Roman period, the Romans based their time on a lunar cycle. However, they didn't know how to add leap months to the year and the months became hopelessly confused with the seasons. Their system was also exploited for political gain, inserting days and even months into their year to keep politicians they favored in office. The chaos brought on an undependable system.

For a while the Romans had experimented with an eight-day cycle (called "nundinum") used mainly for market days and business. They named the days with letters such as A, B, C, etc. Before Christianity, it is generally recognized that the influence of the Jewish seven-day week with its Sabbath rest day was also adopted by the Romans due to its popularity. In fact, for a while in some areas, the two cycles (eight-day and seven-day cycles) ran side by side.[10] However, the Romans used their week as a tool for worshiping their planetary gods. Naming each of the days after heavenly gods spoiled the Creator's meaning behind the Jewish week. The Jews simply identified their days by number to the Sabbath.

The Jewish Sabbath was widely known and became recognized by the Romans as Dies Saturni (Saturday), the weekly day of rest. This certain day that the Jews kept was acceptable to the Romans because they considered this day an unlucky business day anyway. Making Saturday a day for rest and feasting was a great idea to them.

The Jews kept their Sabbath on the seventh day of their weekly cycle. However, because the Romans thought so highly of the day for resting and feasting, Saturday became the first day of their week. This confuses Lunar Sabbatarians into thinking the Romans' week could not have possibly matched up with the Jewish week. Mistakenly they say, "…Sunday did not exist in the Julian calendar of Christ's day. Nor can Saturday be the Biblical seventh-day Sabbath because the pagan planetary week originally began on

Saturday."[11]

But interestingly, history tells us that even though the rest day for Jews and Romans was counted at different times of their defined weeks (seventh day vs. first day) it ended up being the same day. The Romans kept their day religiously on the same day as the Jewish Sabbath for so many years that many Romans were not aware of the Jewish origin.[12] Lunar Sabbatarians don't realize that the Romans got their seven-day week from the Jews themselves. The continuous seven-day weekly cycle did not originate from the pagan Romans.

The correspondence of the Jewish biblical week to the Roman planetary week and modern week cycles are on the following page. This chart makes it clear that the cycles can run congruently. When Emperor Constantine made Sunday the first day of the week in the 4th century AD, the days never moved but still continued to correspond with the biblical week.

"It should be especially noted that the pagan Roman historian [Dio Cassius], in referring to the Sabbath, declared that in 37 BC it was 'the day *even then called the day of Saturn.*' This unmistakably shows that the practice of calling the days after the names of the planetary gods was in some vogue among the Romans *before* the birth of Christ."[13]

A few years earlier, in 46 BC, Julius Caesar had put an end to the long-abused calendar and strived to put it on track with the seasons. The new calendar gave the solar year an

Jewish Biblical Week	Roman Planetary Week	Modern Week
Since Creation	*Since 37 BC*	*Since 4th Century*
1. First day	2. Day of the Sun	1. Sunday
2. Second day	3. Day of the Moon	2. Monday
3. Third day	4. Day of Mars	3. Tuesday
4. Fourth day	5. Day of Mercury	4. Wednesday
5. Fifth day	6. Day of Jupiter	5. Thursday
6. Preparation day	7. Day of Venus	6. Friday
7. Sabbath	1. Day of Saturn	7. Saturday/Sabbath

order by establishing a new dating system, called the Julian calendar. It was based on a luni-solar calendar cycle with the extra days inserted evenly throughout the months. It was fairly accurate astronomically in that it only lost one day every 128 years. So every 128 years the year shifted back one day.

However, the new calendar did not interrupt the weekly cycle. The Romans liked the popular Jewish seven-day week and it eventually won out over the eight-day week. The seven-day weeks drifted through their calendar, the month not starting with any particular day and not having anything to do with the new calendar. The week was a practice by itself, as it is today.

Regardless of how any pagans, whether Assyrians, Babylonians, or Romans, kept their calendars or counted their days, it did not affect the seven-day weekly cycle of the Hebrews. They were given specific instructions to work six days and to rest the seventh. When pagan calendars coincided with the Jewish weekly cycle, it might have been convenient, but it did not affect how they structured their week, as claimed by the Lunar Sabbatarians.

CHRIST'S EXAMPLE

The Julian calendar and the weekly cycle, which the Lunar Sabbatarians call "pagan," was well established by the time Jesus was born. However, there is no record that Jesus ever said anything about the calendar or week being pagan, or that it threatened the foundation of His belief in the Sabbath. He kept the same Sabbath as His fellow Jews and there is evidence that the Sabbath Jesus kept wasn't a Lunar Sabbath. Here is an example of why.

John records Jesus observing the last day of the great Feast (John 7:37). This was the end of the Feast of Tabernacles (John 7:2). The last day occurs on the 22nd of the Jewish month (Leviticus 23:36). To Lunar Sabbatarians, the 22nd is always a Sabbath. However, this is not the case, for John continues by saying the next day Jesus healed a blind man and the Pharisees were angry because it was the Sabbath day (John 8:2, 9:14,15). Jesus obviously did not follow the Lunar Sabbaths because this particular Sabbath day He worshiped on, *fell on the 23rd day.*

THE CONTINUOUS WEEK CONTINUES ON

Since the Jewish and Roman weekly cycles came together the yearly calendar has been changed only once. The Julian calendar, which was in use when Jesus was on earth, continued to be used for fifteen centuries. But because it was not accurate in the length of its year, Pope Gregory initiated a change in the calendar in 1582 by making up for the error in the Julian calendar. Several days were taken from the calendar, yet the weekly cycle was never interrupted.[14]

Even Lunar Sabbatarians and the Vornholts agree that the weekly cycle wasn't interrupted in the change from the Julian into the Gregorian calendar.

> The purpose of the Gregorian calendar was not to change the format of the Julian calendar. It was to bring the date of Easter back into proper alignment with the vernal equinox by removing ten days. This did not alter the cycle of weeks – they flowed smoothly and without interruption from the Julian into the Gregorian.[15]

During the centuries that followed there has never been a change in the days of the week. Sunday back in the days of Constantine, remains Sunday today. The first day of the week today remains the first day since Creation. What a powerful God we serve!

1. Vornholt, eLaine and Vornholt-Jones, Laura Lee. *The Great Calendar Controversy* (Colbert, WA: 4 Angels Publications), p. 11, emphasis supplied.
2. Vornholt, eLaine and Vornholt-Jones, Laura Lee. *History of a Lie* (Colbert, WA: 4 Angels Publications), p. 15.
3. White, Ellen G. *Spiritual Gifts,* Vol. 3, p. 90, emphasis supplied.

4. White, Ellen G. *The Spirit of Prophecy,* Vol. 1, p. 85.1, emphasis supplied.

5. Haynes, Carlyle. *From Sabbath to Sunday,* (Wash. D.C.: Review & Herald, 1928) p. 55.

6. Finley, Mark. *The Almost Forgotten Day,* (Siloam Springs, AR: The Concerned Group, Inc, 1988) pp. 26–27.

7. Ibid.

8. Ibid.

9. Vornholt, *History of a Lie,* p. 12.

10. Bacchiocchi, Samuele. *The Sabbath in the New Testament,* (Michigan: Biblical Perspectives, 1985) p. 187.

11. Vornholt, *History of a Lie,* p. 10.

12. Bacchiocchi, loc. cit., p. 188.

13. Odom, Robert. *Sunday in Roman Paganism,* (Wash. D.C.: Review & Herald, 1944) p. 75.

14. "Has the Calendar Changed?" see http://ecclesia.org/truth/calendar.html.

15. Vornholt, *The Great Calendar Controversy,* p. 72, emphasis supplied.

CHAPTER 5

GOD'S DESIGN OF SEVENS

AN EVENING AND A MORNING

It is interesting when reading the Genesis account about the creation week that every day was called an "evening and morning" except for the seventh day. Why would the seventh day not be called an evening and morning too? A possible reason is that the seventh day was not followed by any more days of creation and didn't need a distinction. The name Sabbath means "cease." It was the end of the week. The formula was set, six separate days and then the seventh[1], no more days, no less. Over and over, the formula is then duplicated.

God took only six days to form and fill our heavens and earth in this manner: three days to form and the next three days to fill.

> In the beginning God created the heavens and the earth, and the earth was without form [Hebrew: unformed] and void [Hebrew: unfilled].[2]

God's orderliness in forming and filling in such a pattern is amazing. Notice the pattern He used in the following chart:

Formed	Filled	Jesus said:
Day 1: Light	Day 4: Sun, Moon, Stars	I am the Light
Day 2: Air, Water	Day 5: Birds, water creatures	I am the Living Water
Day 3: Vegetation	Day 6: Animals, Man	I am the Life

God ceased His work on the seventh day and blessed it as a holy day, calling it the Sabbath of the Lord. Jesus proclaimed, "Come to Me, all you who labor and are heavy laden, and I will give you rest."[3] Jesus *is* rest—the Sabbath is vitally important to God because it reveals Him as our Creator who provides rest.

Almost all mankind has accepted the seven-day weekly cycle, even though there is no similar arrangement in the heavens that would give man reason to decide on the seven-day week as a unit of time. The week is only explained through the influence of the Bible where it is mentioned that in six days God created the world and on the seventh day He rested. This is the only source for the seven-day week.[4]

THE PERFECT NUMBER IN NATURE

The number seven is very prevalent throughout God's Word and nature. It represents completeness and spiritual perfection. It is also known as God's seal or oath.[5] Many things in nature seem to follow a pattern of sevens.[6] Why would there be any question about God designing a continuous weekly cycle of seven days?

Biologically, God made our bodies regulate on a seven-day rhythm. Scientists have discovered that humans do not do well on any other cycle than the consistent seven-day cycle. "Man's pulse beats on the seven-day principle, …six days out of the seven it beats faster in the morning than in the evening, while on the seventh day it beats slower. Thus the number seven is stamped upon physiology…it is interwoven with his very being."[7]

Chronobiologists have discovered several biorhythms in the human body that work on a seven-day cycle such as sleep cycles, heartbeat, blood pressure, and response to infection.[8] The Lunar Sabbath weeks with 8 or 9 days do not fit into these perfect seven-day cycles God has designed.

Mammals and fowls have gestation periods that are exactly divisible by seven. Even a female human's monthly cycle which is normally 28 days is also exactly divisible by seven. Besides this, medical science tells us the human body is renewed cell for cell every seven years.[9]

In nature, there are seven states of matter, seven rows of elements in the periodic table, seven notes in a music scale, seven seas, seven continents, seven colors in a light spectrum, etc.[10] We've seen the perfect use of space in God's design of the beehive—six holes surrounding the seventh.

The number seven seems to indicate God's stamp. Maybe someday we will understand better why.

CYCLES OF SEVEN IN SCRIPTURE

Patterns of seven run throughout the entire Bible more than any other number.[11] There is an abundance of sevens, with over 50 occurrences in the book of Revelation alone: heavens, thrones, seals, churches, angels, spirits of God, lampstands, thunders, heads, horns, eyes, golden bowls, stars, crowns, mountains, and kings.[12] Jesus spoke seven "I am" statements in the gospels, God instituted seven annual feasts that were to be repeated every year and the Creator also made a seventh-day weekly Sabbath.

In copying God's Word in the Hebrew or Greek, ancient scribes were extremely careful in its accuracy by counting the letters, words, and phrases forwards and backwards. In these languages the letters were also used to indicate numbers so the numeric value of a word was the total of all its letters. Amazingly, words and sentences in the book of Genesis were always divisible by seven.[13]

For example, just the first verse of the Bible, "In the beginning God created the heaven and the earth,"[14] contains over 30 different combinations of seven.[15] The verse has seven Hebrew words with a total of 28 letters (4x7). The numeric value of just the three nouns "God," "heaven," and "earth" has a total of 777. This triple number is often an expression of complete or total meaning.[16]

In the Sanctuary, bread was to be kept continually on the table of shewbread in the holy place. Every Sabbath the priests were to place fresh bread upon the table. It was to remain on the table a week (seven days). Then it was taken off the table the next Sabbath and eaten by the priests. This symbolized the added spiritual blessing we can receive from God's Word every Sabbath day.[17] If there were extra unaccounted-for days as in the Lunar Sabbath theory, the priests would have gone hungry waiting for the next batch of bread, or there should have been written instructions on what to do differently on those days, but there isn't.

God gave a clear example of sevens through the sabbatical seasons.[18] Every seven years was considered a sabbath for the land, and after seven of these "seven-year" sabbaths came the Year of Jubilee. Both institutions rested on the cycle of seven, as did the weekly Sabbath, and both were "a Sabbath of solemn rest to the land, a Sabbath to the Lord."[19]

Ellen White tells us that our world is about 6000 years old. Our life here on earth is to bring blessing to others and glorify God in everything we do. Humanity has had 6000 years to see the results of following Satan's method of government. Jesus is coming soon and we will be spending the seventh 1000 years in peace and rest with Him before we come back to this earth made new. It is a millennial sabbath for all God's people!

THE SEVEN-DAY WEEK

A major cycle of sevens is the 70-week prophecy that foretold the Messiah's death in 31 AD. The only way to understand how the final week of the 70-week prophecy found in Daniel 9:24–27 ended in 27–34 AD, is to understand that a week is a cycle of seven.

Every place in the Daniel 9 prophecy where the word "week" is found, the original Hebrew word is *"shabuwa."* Strong's concordance defines *shabuwa* as: "sevened," i.e. a week (specifically, of years) "seven, week." The word "week" found anywhere in the Bible means seven. The seventy sevens equal 490 days/years. If a week was sometimes eight or nine days as in the Lunar Sabbath theory, the cycle of seventy sevens/eights/nines would not point us to 31 AD. This prophecy only works with precise cycles of seven.

No one can say there is an "eight-day week," because the formula is a week = seven days. Words that have specific numerical meaning can't be used otherwise. Using the rules of language, for instance, the following are impossible: a five-person quartet, a four-member Trinity, a ninety-year century, a twelve-sided octagon, a ten-egg dozen, a six-cent nickel, an eight-day week…

Another good example of a continuous weekly cycle is when God fed the Hebrews manna in the wilderness. For five days He gave them only enough manna for the day. If they kept some overnight, it would spoil. On the sixth day, they were to gather a *double portion*—for the sixth day and for the Sabbath day. This time it didn't spoil and it lasted through the holy day. There never was more or less than what God specified, otherwise the Hebrews would go hungry. There was no mention of collecting triple or quadruple for "long weekends," two Sabbath days together—only the pattern for a seven-day week. This cycle repeated itself for over 40 years. God was faithful in His care!

COUNT TO PENTECOST

The greatest obstacle for those who insist the continuous weekly cycle is pagan, is how the Lunar Sabbath theory conflicts with calculating the Feast of Weeks.

Fifty days after the Passover weekend of Jesus' death and resurrection was the feast of Pentecost. This time period is the Feast of Weeks. Israel was told to count seven Sabbaths or continuous weeks from the day after the Sabbath that occurs during the Feast of Unleavened Bread. After the seven sevens (49), if we count to the day after the seventh Sabbath or week, we would have counted 50 days:

> And you shall count for yourselves from the day after the Sabbath, [meaning the seventh-day Sabbath] from the day that you brought the sheaf of the wave offering: seven Sabbaths shall be completed. Count fifty days to the day after the seventh Sabbath; then you shall offer a new grain offering to the Lord.[20]

How does this work for a Lunar Sabbatarian? The following charts demonstrate how the count of seven Sabbaths and 50 days happens with the Lunar Sabbath theory compared to the continuous weekly cycle. The small numbers below the days count the days to Pentecost. The underlined numbers are Sabbaths.

The first chart is the Lunar Sabbath calendar with the extra new moon "Sabbaths" and one "non-day." The fiftieth day does not fall on "the day after the seventh Sabbath."

The Feast of Weeks does not fit at all into the Lunar Sabbath model. The fact is, counting 50 days on a Lunar calendar does not allow Pentecost to land the day after the seventh Sabbath.[21] Lunar Sabbatarians answer this problem by saying that you cannot count the "non-days" or new moon days into the equation when counting to Pentecost. They must have some mystical way to make these days disappear when it is convenient for their theory.

The only way counting to Pentecost can logically work is

Lunar Sabbaths Month-Nisan/Iyar 31 AD

	9	10	11	12	13	14	_15_	
	16 (1)	17 (2)	18 (3)	19 (4)	20 (5)	21 (6)	_22_ (7)	
	23 (8)	24 (9)	25 (10)	26 (11)	27 (12)	28 (13)	_29_ (14)	30 (15)
_1_ (16)	2 (17)	3 (18)	4 (19)	5 (20)	6 (21)	7 (22)	_8_ (23)	
	9 (24)	10 (25)	11 (26)	12 (27)	13 (28)	14 (29)	_15_ (30)	
	16 (31)	17 (32)	18 (33)	19 (34)	20 (35)	21 (36)	_22_ (37)	
	23 (38)	24 (39)	25 (40)	26 (41)	27 (42)	28 (43)	_29_ (44)	
_1_ (45)	2 (46)	3 (47)	4 (48)	5 (49)	6 (50)	7	_8_	

←Sabbath before start of Feasts of Weeks (row 1)

←Seventh Sabbath after wave sheaf offering (row 8)

by just plainly counting seven "sevens" or continuous weeks as the Bible says to do. In this we can be sure that the seven-day weekly cycle is a continuous cycle.

What the Lord commanded for Pentecost fits perfectly into continuous seven-day weeks. The fiftieth day comes the day after the seventh "seven" following the feast. The following chart demonstrates how the count to Pentecost works with the continuous seven-day weekly cycle.

In all these examples, the number seven seems to show a distinct pattern of our Creator. God, in His wisdom, provided a simple number to seal His Sabbath. The Lunar Sabbath weeks with 8 or 9 days (counting the "non-days" and new moon Sabbath days) do not fit into the perfect pattern.

Scriptural
Continuous Weeks-Nisan/Iyar 31 AD

9	10	11	12	13	14	15	←Sabbath before start of Feasts of Weeks
16 (1)	17 (2)	18 (3)	19 (4)	20 (5)	21 (6)	22 (7)	
23 (8)	24 (9)	25 (10)	26 (11)	27 (12)	28 (13)	29 (14)	
30 (15)	1 (16)	2	3 (18)	4 (19)	5 (20)	6 (21)	
7 (22)	8 (23)	9 (24)	10 (25)	11 (26)	12 (27)	13 (28)	
14 (29)	15 (30)	16 (31)	17 (32)	18 (33)	19 (34)	20 (35)	
21 (36)	22 (37)	23 (38)	24 (39)	25 (40)	26 (41)	27 (42)	
28 (43)	29 (44)	30 (45)	1 (46)	2 (47)	3 (48)	4 (49)	←Seventh Sabbath after wave sheaf offering
Pentecost → 5 (50)							

1. Bacchiocchi, Samuele. "A New Attack Against The Sabbath – Part 3", (December 12, 2001), see biblicalperspectives.com/endtimeissues/.

2. Genesis 1:1.

3. Matthew 11:28.

4. Fine, Larry. "The Jewish Calendar," *The Jewish Magazine,* see jewishmag. co.il/86mag.

5. Newman, Keith. "Is God a Mathematician?," see wordworx.co.nz/panin. html.

6. Tan, Enoch. "Seven in Science and Nature," (August 2006) see library. thinkquest.org/06aug/00922.

7. Ibid.

8. Duncan, David. *Calendar,* (New York: Avon Books, Inc., 1998) p. 46.

9. Newman, op. cit.

10. Tan, op. cit.

11. Harris, Andrew. "Seven," (August 21, 2001) see vic.australis.com.au/ hazz/number007.html.

12. Newman, op. cit.

13. Gray, Jonathan. "The Amazing 'Weapon' Discovery," *Update International,* (February–April 2010).

14. Genesis 1:1.

15. Gray, op. cit.

16. Newman, op. cit.

17. Haskell, Stephen. *Story of Daniel the Prophet,* (New York, NY: Bible Training School, 1995) p. 269.

18. Leviticus 25:4.

19. Goldstein, Clifford. *Like a Fire in my Bones,* (Idaho: Pacific Press, 1998), p. 183.

20. Leviticus 23:15–16.

21. Eliyah, "Beware of the Lunar Sabbath," see eliyah.com.

CHAPTER 6

IS SATURDAY THE SABBATH?

A CRITICAL ISSUE

The Vornholts say that Jesus, the apostles, and the ancient Jews kept the Lunar Sabbath–not the Saturday of the "pagan weekly cycle." They state,

> Sunday is not the only worship day founded upon paganism. Saturday, *dies Saturni*, as the original first day of the pagan week, is also a counterfeit. As the seventh day of the modern week, it is a counterfeit for the true seventh-day Sabbath of the Bible.[1]

We agree with the Vornholts that both Jesus and the Christian apostles kept the "true" Sabbath. However, we disagree on how the true Sabbath is determined. There is only one true Sabbath; the other is false. It stands to reason that if ancient historical documents show that the Jews did indeed keep a weekly Sabbath on the same day the Romans termed Saturn's day, then the Lunar Sabbath theory would dissolve.

SABBATH TORCH NEVER LOST

James Arrabito, a Seventh-day Adventist, was an extensive scholar of the Sabbath. He believed that if Ellen White was right about men keeping the true Sabbath through all the ages, then he should be able to find proof through old writings and customs since the death of Jesus. If the Lunar Sabbath theory was truly observed, there should instead be ample evidence of it throughout the world where Jews and early Christians had spread. Ellen White comments,

> In every age there were witnesses for God—men who cherished faith in Christ as the only mediator between God and man, who held the Bible as the only rule of life, and who hallowed the true Sabbath. How much the world owes to these men, posterity will never know. They were branded as heretics, their motives impugned, their characters maligned, their writings suppressed, misrepresented, or mutilated. Yet, they stood firm, and from age to age maintained their faith in its purity, as a sacred heritage for the generations to come.[2]

James Arrabito discovered the true Sabbath, kept continually through every century in isolated places all over the world, was observed on the same day as the Roman Saturday. James died several years ago but all of the information of his discoveries had been sketched into a final draft for a video series. His wife Pat took on the project and a set of 5 DVD's, *The Seventh Day*, resulted. It traces the history of the true Sabbath from creation and shows there never was a break in its true observance from the time of Christ.[3]

Faithful followers since the time of Jesus were forced to retreat to isolated places because of persecution. They took the unadulterated translation of the Bible with them and loyally kept the Sabbath torch burning. They held to the truth for over 1000 years and in so doing had preserved the true seventh-day Sabbath and the Word of God, the two most important witnesses of God.[4]

CHRIST AND THE APOSTLES

One of Jesus' reforms was to free the Sabbath from the burdensome traditions of the Pharisees. He kept the Sabbath as God had intended and taught His people how to keep it. A few years after His death, the apostles took the gospel from the Jewish nation to the Gentile people who were ready for it. The Gentiles wanted the heart-changing freedom Jesus promised.

Naturally, as the Gentiles became Christians, they worshipped on the true Sabbath. We're given this evidence in the book of Acts.

> So when the Jews went out of the synagogue, the Gentiles begged that these words might be preached to them the next Sabbath.[5]

> And he reasoned in the synagogue every Sabbath, and persuaded both Jews and Greeks.[6]

The Gentiles observed the Sabbath, but the Bible never said it was an issue for them. Would this be because the Gentiles were in some way already observing the day

(Saturday)? If the Apostles had been keeping the Lunar Sabbath and the Romans were following the work week of the Julian calendar, Sabbath-keeping would have been a problem for both the Jews and the Gentile Christians and the issue would have been addressed in Scripture. But there is no indication of such a problem in the New Testament or in other early Christian literature.[7]

In the first century AD, Christianity pervaded all known nations as the disciples of Christ went into all the world spreading the gospel. The influence of the apostles and early Christians was powerful, for it appears that Sabbath observance was acceptable to all peoples and nations. The observance of a Sunday feast day was not even in practice yet.[8] "…the true Sabbath had been kept by all Christians. They were jealous for the honor of God, and, believing that His law is immutable, they zealously guarded the sacredness of its precepts."[9]

The famous historian, Josephus, stated, "There is not any city of the Grecians, nor any of the barbarians, nor any nation whatsoever, whither our custom of resting on the seventh day hath not come!"[10] It wasn't until the second century (after 100 AD) that any concrete evidence of Sunday observance arose anywhere.[11]

SATURN'S DAY

The Jews fought against and persecuted the Christians and their faith. The Jews took advantage of the instability of the Roman Empire and revolted against Roman authority in 66 AD, taking over complete control of Jerusalem. Their obnoxious behavior caused many to hate them. The reason the Sabbath was still accepted during this time was not due to the Jews, but because the Christians upheld it faithfully.

The Romans sensed that the pride of the Jews was in their temple. So in 70 AD the Romans attacked Jerusalem and burned the temple to the ground. Because of a warning Jesus gave years before, the Christians fled and safely escaped.

Referring to the fall of Jerusalem, a Roman soldier and writer, Sextus Julius Frontinus, wrote that they "...attacked the Jews on the day of Saturn, on which it is forbidden for them to do anything serious, and defeated them."[12]

First century Roman historian Dio Cassius' account is very much the same, "Thus was Jerusalem destroyed on the very day of Saturn, the day which even now the Jews reverence most."[13]

This is unmistakeable evidence that the Sabbath day kept by the Jews was on the day known as Saturn's Day (Saturday) to the Romans. The Romans attacked on a Saturday specifically because they knew the Jewish people wouldn't be ready to defend themselves on their holy Sabbath day. Still within the time frame of the life of John, the beloved disciple of Jesus, we have strong evidence that the "Saturday" Sabbath, not a Lunar Sabbath, was the true Sabbath.

TERTULLIAN

Tertullian, a Christian apologist around 200 AD, reproached the pagans for having adopted the custom of resting on the "Jewish" Sabbath. He wrote,

> You have selected one day (Saturday) in preference to other days as the day on which you do not take a bath or you postpone it until the evening, and on which you devoted yourselves to leisure and abstain from revelry. In so doing you are turning from your own religion to a foreign religion, for the Sabbath and special supper are Jewish ceremonial observances.[14]

Tertullian happened to observe Sunday in celebration of Christ's resurrection.

> Likewise, if we devote the day of the Sun to festivity (from a far different reason from Sun worship), we are in a second place from those who devote the day of Saturn to rest and eating, themselves also deviating by way of a Jewish custom of which they are ignorant.[15]

Tertullian compares menial Christians who worshiped on Sunday in a similar way to sun worshippers as being worse than those who rested on Saturday like the Jews. They were doing it, but didn't really know why.

If Tertullian and others were observing the Sunday festivities because of the resurrection of Jesus, then we know Sunday is the first day of the Jewish week because that is when scriptures tell us He arose. And if Tertullian acclaimed that the day of Saturn was the day the Jews kept holy, then here is yet another confirmation that the Jewish Sabbath occurred on the day known as Saturn's day. Remembering that Tertullian wrote during the time period when Lunar Sabbatarians still feel the "true" Sabbath was in place, these details are strong indications that the true Sabbath is based on the weekly cycle.

It should be said that even though the Sabbath occurred on the pagan Saturday, Christians never considered worshiping on a pagan day. It was a sacred day that pagans defiled by naming it after pagan deities. Christians refused to call their Sabbath by the pagan god, Saturn. Sabbath was created by the true God before the pagans tainted it. Every day of the week had pagan connotations. If a holy day could have happened on any of those days the pagan origins would have been ignored by the Christians.

Here is yet another bit of evidence the Sabbath was on Saturday.

> In the beginning of the Roman Church of the fourth century a Roman Bishop, Sylvester the first, [unsuccessfully] directed that the names of the days of the week be changed. Rather than being called by pagan gods, they should be numbered, except for Sunday, which should be designated as "The Lord's Day" and Saturday, which would continue to be called "The Sabbath."[16]

LITERATURE CONFIRMATION

Another example from first century literature comes from Roman historians and writers. In 100 AD, the Historian

Cornelius Tacitus suggested that Jews kept the Sabbath out of laziness. He also associated the Sabbath with the Roman idol, Saturn, "They are said to have devoted the seventh day to rest, because that day brought an end to their troubles. Later, finding idleness alluring, they gave up the seventh year as well to sloth. Others maintain that they do this in honor of Saturn."[17] Here is a pagan indicating that the Sabbath was concurrent with the Romans' week day named after Saturn—Saturday.

A Jew, Philo Judaeus, writes about his definition of what Sabbath meant to the Jews, "The fourth commandment has reference to the sacred seventh day, that it may be passed in a sacred and holy manner. …the nation of the Jews keeps every seventh day regularly, after each interval of six days."[18] This could not refer to a Lunar Sabbath system because there would have to be some intervals in other than a regular seven-day cycle.

By the few examples given, we see that throughout history both Jewish and non-Jewish sources confirm the truth that the seventh-day weekly Sabbath does in fact fall on the Roman Saturday.

GREAT BRITAIN

The civilized nation of Great Britain wasn't pursued by Rome until 597 AD. When Roman missionaries arrived they were amazed that Britain had already embraced Christianity for over 500 years. It was pure and untainted.

In Great Britain, primitive Christianity had very early taken root. The gospel received by the Britons in the first centuries, was then uncorrupted by Romish apostasy. Persecution from pagan emperors, which extended even to these far-off shores, was the only gift that the first churches of Britain received from Rome. Many of the Christians, fleeing from persecution in England, found refuge in Scotland; thence the truth was carried to Ireland, and in all these countries it was received with gladness.[19]

A document found stated the gospel came to Britain in the last year of Tiberius Caesar. That was only six years after the resurrection of Jesus. Who could have told this nation about Jesus?

Many more documents told how an exiled Joseph of Arimathea with several others made their way to Britain to share the good news. About a hundred and sixty disciples were sent later to assist Joseph and his companions. Though Christianity was privately confessed elsewhere, Great Britain became the first nation to receive and accept Christianity as their religion.[20]

As the Roman church expanded its borders it took in Britain as well. Many in Britain kept both Saturday and Sunday as rest days—Sunday because of the Roman influences and Saturday because, "It seems to have been customary in the Celtic churches of early time to keep Saturday, the Jewish Sabbath as a day of rest from labor. They obeyed the fourth commandment literally upon the seventh day of the week."[21]

A nation that remained pure for over 500 years should

be positive evidence as to what the true Sabbath day was. If they had received the gospel directly from an immediate disciple of Jesus, including the seventh-day Sabbath then we know they kept the Sabbath on the day known as Saturday long before the pagan Roman influence arrived.

LANGUAGES AND CULTURES

Another interesting detail concerning Saturday being the Sabbath is how nations worldwide, totally unrelated to each other, and many of them enemies of each other, have named their days of the week.

Over a hundred years ago William Jones, a Seventh-day Baptist, put together a chart of approximately 160 countries and the names for their days of the week and how they matched up with the ancient Jewish week.

Interestingly, in some of the nations that held onto the planetary names of the days, Saturday fell on the same day as the seventh-day Sabbath. The nations have used these names of the weeks for centuries, since Christianity inhabited the world. This is just one more confirmation the early Christians regarded the Sabbath from the biblical continuous weekly cycle.[22]

The finding was, "In more than 100 languages the word for the seventh-day [sic] of the week is the national word for Sabbath."[23] Here are just a few examples:

Ancient Syriac: Shabatho

Babylonian:	Sabatu
Armenian:	Shapat
Polynesian:	Hari sabtu
Swahili:	Assabt
Latin:	Sabbatum
Italian:	Sabbato
Spanish:	Sabado
Russian:	Subbota
Assyrian:	Sabata
Georgian:	Shabati

1. Vornholt, eLaine and Vornholt-Jones, Laura Lee. *History of a Lie* (Colbert, WA: 4 Angels Publications), p. 30.

2. White, Ellen G. *The Great Controversy,* p. 61.

3. Wood, Jim, *The Seventh Day,* (Angwin, CA: LLT Productions, 2002).

4. White, loc. cit., pp. 61–78.

5. Acts 13:42.

6. Acts 18:4.

7. Eliyah, "Beware of the Lunar Sabbath," see eliyah.com.

8. Finley, Mark. *The Almost Forgotten Day,* (Arkansas, Concerned Group, 1988) p. 58.

9. White, loc. cit., p. 52.

10. Finley, loc. cit., p. 60.

11. Strand, Kenneth. *The Sabbath in Scripture and History,* (Review & Herald Pub, 1982) p. 330.

12. Bacchiocchi, Samuele. "A New Attack Against The Sabbath – Part 3," (December 12, 2001).

13. Bacchiochi, loc. cit.

14. Bacchiochi, loc. cit.

15. Odom, Robert. *Sunday in Roman Paganism,* p. 110–111.

16. Odom, Robert. *Sabbath and Sunday in Early Christianity,* (Wash. D.C.: Review & Herald, 1977), p. 301, emphasis supplied.

17. Ibid, From *The Histories,* Book V.

18. Ibid. *The Decalogue,* XX, p. 526.

19. White, loc. cit., p. 62.

20. Gray, Jonathan. *Ark of the Covenant,* (Thorsby, AL: SHM Productions Inc., 1997) pp. 316–321.

21. Moffat, James. "The Church in Scotland," as quoted in *The Seventh Day,* (Angwin, CA: LLT Productions, 2002).

22. Jones, William. *A Chart of the Week,* see seventh-day.org/chartweek.

23. Vandeman, George. *When God Made Rest,* (Idaho: Pacific Press, 1987), p. 31.

CHAPTER 7

LUNAR SABBATH LOST?

LUNAR SABBATH EVAPORATES?

Around the fourth century, the Vornholts believe there was a disruptive calendar change caused by Roman Emperor Constantine which suddenly forced the Lunar Sabbath out of existence. This in turn forced the Jews to give up their "Biblical Sabbath" which the Vornholts interpret to mean the Lunar Sabbath.

They state, "The persecution following legislation [Emperor Constantine attempted to legalize Easter to yearly fall on a Sunday] which forbade the 'Jewish computation of the calendar' was so extreme that, in the end, the Jews gave up their calendar handed down from Creation…"[1]

The idea that "…by their own admission, the Jews deliberately and knowingly changed their calendar by which the true Sabbath was calculated,"[2] makes it sound like the Sabbath was given up because it was tied to the seasonal feast calendar, which it was not.

There is no evidence that because of Constantine's Easter Sunday legislation in the fourth century, Jews were forced to give up a calendar or the Sabbath. Perhaps the Vornholts are referring to a conflict that happened in the second century.

THE WAR WITH ROME

History says that in the second century the Jews living in Palestine were at war with the Romans. The Jews were beaten down and very few in Palestine survived. To make sure there were no more uprisings by the Jews, the Romans forced them to leave Jerusalem and it was given to the Gentiles. The Jews were also forbidden to study the Torah, carry out any religious rites, or to keep the Sabbath day on punishment of death.

Though a few chose to suffer death rather then be disloyal to God, the majority of Jews remaining near Jerusalem ended up desecrating the Sabbath. Because the persecution continued, the few highest ranking Jewish leaders met and decided to establish a strange pronouncement. It was voted that all Jewish laws could be broken to avoid death by torture except idolatry, adultery, and murder.

When the Jews realized their Sanhedrin in Jerusalem was going to be disbanded, they calculated all the new moons and religious feasts for the next 4000 years and made the proper declarations for all of them. Though the accuracy of this calculation is doubtful, Jews still use this to celebrate the feasts today.[3]

This must be what the Vornholts were referring to when they said, "By establishing a fixed calendar based on his authority as president of the Sanhedrin, Hillel II set aside the original calendar…"[4] However, the problem occurs when they suppose that the Saturday/Sabbath was also adjusted as part of the "new" fixed calendar. Again, this idea comes from the assumption that the Sabbath is part of the luni-solar calendar.

The Christian church in the first centuries, which was comprised of mainly Jewish Christians before the war with the Romans, was now made up of mostly Gentiles. The emperor ordered soldiers to keep constant guard to prevent any Jews from approaching Jerusalem. However, the Gentile Christians were free to continue keeping the same Biblical Sabbath the Jews from Jerusalem had to abandon.

The Vornholts claim that, "[the Jews] did not know when the true Sabbath occurred."[5] (On the other hand, they also say "It is true that the Jews have never lost track of the true Sabbath.")[6] The large number of Jews living all over the world were not affected by the Roman ban on the Sabbath near Jerusalem. "[They] spread abroad from the land at various periods in time. When one looks to the nations to see what day they keep holy, the historical fact is, every group of Jews keeps the same sequence of days, and the same Sabbath."[7]

Because of faithful Jews from around the world we have more than scientific and historical evidence for the continuous weekly Sabbath. "Every other Near East ethnic group has disappeared—the Hittites, Canaanites, Amorites, Amalekites, Perizzites, Jebusites, Sumarians, Babylonians,

Assyrians, Moabites, Philistines—but the Jews remain and, with them, the seventh-day Sabbath."[8] They have faithfully kept it since the time of Moses, 3500 years ago, and have continued to keep track of the Sabbath each week. And it is passed down from generation to generation.

Any Jew today will tell you that the seventh day is the Sabbath, and that it falls on the Saturday of each week. Moreover, since God has commanded us to worship on the Sabbath day to show allegiance to Him, don't you think He would preserve its identity?"[9]

THE MISSING LINK

Have you noticed that one of the biggest challenges to the Evolution theory is that there are missing links between all types of living beings which are supposed to be related to each other? There are no transitional forms between pigs and horses, reptiles and birds, or even apes and humans. In reality, if the evolutionary theory were true, with millions of transitions and millions of years of evolving, there would be millions of progressive links everywhere. There should even be transitional forms living today—but there are none.

Likewise with the Lunar Sabbath debate. If the Jews were forced to give up a Lunar Sabbath to use the pagan calendar instead, there should be huge amounts of evidence in existence today that this change occurred. Changing from following the Sabbath by observing moon cycles to a continuous weekly cycle is a gigantic shift in practice and belief.

There would be records everywhere in history about the resistance of the Jews in changing their method of keeping Sabbath. Since the Jews spread throughout the nations of the world, if the Lunar Sabbath theory were true, it would have required vast armies and missionaries going everywhere to convince and enforce the change of Jewish Sabbath-keeping from the lunar method to the pagan weekly cycle. Today, there should still be pockets of orthodox Jewish groups worldwide ferociously clinging to the old ways of keeping the "Biblical Lunar Sabbath."

But the exact opposite is true. History is absolutely silent as to such events taking place. There are no recorded commands given to change Sabbath observance from a lunar to weekly cycle. Today, Jews spread around the world keep the Sabbath on Saturday.

Any attempt to disturb the seven-day cycle has always aroused most determined opposition of the Jewish authorities…" [The Royal Greenwich Observatory in London, England continues this thought with,] "…we are quite certain that no such disturbance has ever been put into effect."[10]

> All that we have discovered is confirmed by the testimony of millions of Jews who over two millennia since Christ have zealously observed the Sabbath. Dispersed throughout the world, they all keep the same day. And when they assemble, even though there may be disputes on the proper way to observe it, there is never a dispute on when to observe Shabbat. It begins Friday night at sundown and ends Saturday night at sundown.

No other single fact of history can claim the degree of certainty of the Sabbath. No historian, whether religious or secular, disputes the fact that the Sabbath observed by Christ is Saturday.[11]

Think of the mathematical odds of all the Jews worldwide, at the same time, changing their God-given foundational heritage. Add to this the huge blank in the historical record of anything of the kind occurring. The chances of this happening are impossible. This cannot be swept away with "that is not an important point." This is an overwhelming missing link for the Lunar Sabbath theory.

FIRST CENTURY LITERATURE

A modern Jewish-Christian historian who goes by the name Eliyah,[12] researched first century literature to discover if there was any historical evidence for the Jews keeping a Lunar Sabbath or a regular weekly Sabbath as we know it today. He did not find any evidence of a Lunar Sabbath in Jewish history. Here is some historical evidence he found to substantiate the seventh-day Sabbath occurring on Saturday.

The first reference comes out of the Talmud. Eliyah made it clear that he did not believe in following the Talmud or using it for authoritative doctrine, but it is a great resource for the history of that time period. Though compiled about 130 years after the destruction of Jerusalem, it was written around the time of Christ.

One of the parts of the Talmud called the Mishnah

often contained opposing views of two Jewish scholars called Shammai and Hillel. They lived before and after the time of Christ, so their outlook gives a good idea of what Jesus would have experienced and religiously observed. One dispute between the two was about what blessing needed to be recited *if* the "new moon falls on a Sabbath."

> The New Moon is different from a festival…if a New Moon falls on a Sabbath, Beth Shammai ruled: One recites in his additional prayer eight benedictions and Beth Hillel ruled: Seven? This is indeed a difficulty. *Talmud* - Mas. Eiruvin 40b[13]

If the Jews kept a Lunar Sabbath, this would have never been an issue because the new moon would never fall on a seventh-day Lunar Sabbath. It is obvious that even though the two scholars disagreed on many things, they did not observe the Lunar Sabbath.

Another example in the Mishnah states what the priests did with the non-meat portions of the Passover Lamb:

> The bones, and the sinews, and the nothar of the paschal lamb are to be burnt on the sixteenth. If the sixteenth falls on the Sabbath, they are to be burnt on the seventeenth, because they do not override either the Sabbath or the festival. *Talmud* - Pesachim 83a[14]

Again, because the Lunar Sabbath never falls on the sixteenth day, this must be referring to a continuous seven-day weekly Sabbath, independent of the moon. It also shows that the dates of the Sabbath fluctuated because sometimes special days would land on the Sabbath and sometimes it wouldn't.

Eliyah mentioned that, "…if you ever read the Talmud in depth, you will come away with one clear impression: They debated about almost everything. Something as major as a change in when the Sabbath is observed ought to have been at least debated somewhere. After all, they debated every little fine point of the law! The lack of such a debate speaks volumes."[15]

The Dead Sea Scrolls, rediscovered in caves near the Dead Sea in the mid-twentieth century, added credibility to our Bible in the minds of many who questioned its historicity. Said to be authored by the Essenes, a Jewish sect of the first century, the scrolls describe the Essenes' beliefs and practices.

Eliyah says about the Essenes, "It is generally undisputed (even by Lunar Sabbatarians) that the authors of these scrolls did not keep a Lunar Sabbath. Rather, the Calendrical scroll shows that they observed a recurring seven-day weekly cycle, independent of the moon phases. I know of no one who disputes this. Of course, Lunar Sabbatarians generally will teach that this Jewish sect was wrong about the Sabbath.[16]

Josephus, a well known Jewish historian of Judean life in the first century, wrote a great deal about the Essenes' practices being different from other Jews. But as far as the Sabbath, he stated, "…they are stricter than any other of the Jews in resting from their labors on the seventh day."[17]

THE JEWISH SPLIT

When strong differences arise between two groups, a split generally occurs, with some believing one way and others believing the other way. With such conflicting changes to the belief structure of the Jews, we should see such a split among them regarding how to keep the Sabbath.

History shows no disagreement to the reckoning of the Sabbath day, only about the keeping of it. The Essenes had split off from the main Jewish groups and were critical of the Jews on many things, but not which day was the true Sabbath. If the Essenes kept a continuous weekly Sabbath, then all the Jewish sects must have observed the same day.

A major split between Jewish groups did occur later, but it wasn't over the Sabbath issue. It was the split between the Karaite and Rabbinical Jews—and one major difference was how to calculate the feast days.

From the time of Christ, the Karaite Jews faithfully reckoned feast days by observation from Jerusalem. The Rabbinical Jews, content with living in different countries, used calculation to determine when to keep the feasts.

Even with these differences, both groups of Jews still kept Saturday as the Sabbath. The Karaite Jews, with their meticulous zeal in observing God's laws, should still have strong evidence for keeping the Sabbath by lunar observation if they ever did, but there is no documentation about them ever keeping a Lunar Sabbath.

MULTIPLE TIME CYCLES

When I presented to the Vornholts the fact that the Jewish luni-solar cycle and weekly cycle were two separate time cycles, their response indicated that it was not possible for the Jews to calculate both a lunar month and a seven-day week at the same time. However, it is possible. During the lifetime of Jesus the Jews observed at least four different time cycles.

The "Jewish civil cycle" ended the year in the autumn and was considered the Jewish New Year. The "sacred calendar," in which the new moons and feasts were observed religiously, started in the spring. Both these cycles were based on the moon.[18] By this time, the Jews also followed the Romans' "imperial civil calendar" (the Julian calendar) for civic matters that pertained to the payment of taxes and dealing with government officials.[19] The last cycle was the "seven-day weekly cycle," independent of any known celestial motion and occurring on a weekly basis. It originally was not part of any calendar but stood alone as a witness to God's power.

Is it possible to function with more than one "time cycle" at a time? Is your memory good enough to distinguish between a "biblical day" (sunset to sunset) and a "legal day" (midnight to midnight)? Don't we already function with the "work week" of Monday through Friday versus a "legal week" of Sunday through Saturday? Nobody seems to find it too difficult to understand the various year cycles like a "school year" (September through June) in comparison to a "tax year" (April 16 through April 15) and also the "calendar year" (January through December)? We do it all the time. There are also "fiscal years," "business years," "church officer years," and the like that people observe without much trouble. No, it is not inconsistent to have more than one time cycle.

Does it seem odd that God may have used the pagan Romans to assist in preserving the weekly cycle and the understanding of His Sabbath? Throughout the Bible, God used pagan nations to do His work numerous times. He used the Philistines, the Assyrians, the Babylonians, and others to teach and discipline His people when they went astray. In turn, people from these nations were influenced by His people.

Even now the Roman calendar marks the seventh day of the week to coincide with the Sabbath. God had preserved it with the Jews down to the time of Christ and passed the torch of the weekly Sabbath down through the centuries to the faithful Christians of modern times. If something is as important as the Sabbath to God, why wouldn't He keep it pure all these years?

1. Vornholt, eLaine and Vornholt-Jones, Laura Lee. *History of a Lie* (Colbert, WA: 4 Angels Publications), p. 27.

2. Vornholt, loc. cit., p. 27.

3. "The New Moon and the Power of Judaism," see beingjewish.com

4. Vornholt, loc. cit., p. 28.

5. Vornholt, loc. cit., p. 28.

6. Vornholt, loc. cit., p. 27–28.

7. Webster, Hutton. *Rest Days: A Study in Early Law and Morality,* (New York: MacMillan Comp., 1916) p. 244–245.

8. "Has the Calendar Been Changed?" see ecclesia.org/truth/calendar. html.

9. See ecclesia.org/truth/calendar.html.

10. Finley, Mark. *The Almost Forgotten Day,* p. 26, 27.

11. "The Sabbath," see www.bibleonly.org.

12. Eliyah, "Beware of the Lunar Sabbath," see eliyah.com.

13. Ibid.

14. Ibid.

15. Ibid.

16. Ibid.

17. Ibid. Josephus, Wars of the Jews 2:147.

18. Stephen Haskell, *The Cross and Its Shadow,* p. 240.

19. "The Hebrew Calendar", see wikipedia.com.

THE SABBATH TAKES A TURN

COUNCIL OF NICAEA

Continuing on with the Vornholts' belief in a disruptive calendar change in the fourth century, their first point was that the Lunar Sabbath was forced out of existence. A second point was that Emperor Constantine made a legislation that forced Jews into the Roman calendar mold. This legislation was supposed to have been made at what was called the Council of Nicaea.

The Council of Nicaea holds significant importance to the Vornholt's theory. It is the foundation of how they believe the Lunar Sabbath was eliminated in history and lost for generations. The Council of Nicaea supposedly caused enforcement of the pagan weekly cycle and pagan Saturday Sabbath by default. Here are a few of their statements.

The foundation laid by Constantine's "Sunday law" is the reason why Saturday and Sunday keepers worship on the days they do. The decrees of Nicaea legislated into place an entire counterfeit system of religion with its pagan solar calendar. Thus the knowledge of the Creator's calendar with *His true seventh-day Sabbath has been buried under the accumulated weight of centuries of continuously cycling weeks.*[1]

Emperor Constantine, at the Council of Nicaea, changed both paganism and Christianity by combining them into a new organism. *The true luni-solar calendar was forcibly eliminated and the pagan/Julian calendar with its continuous cycle of weeks was exalted and supported by the Church/State.*[2]

The change of the calendar took place at the Council of Nicaea in 321 AD. *The very first Sunday law was a law that outlawed the Biblical luni-solar calendar and substituted the pagan Julian calendar in its place.*[3]

Such statements do not seem to match history. The reason for the Council of Nicaea in 325 AD (not 321 AD as stated) was to deal with arguments which had simmered for several years concerning Jesus Christ. Many creeds were also made concerning how elders were to behave and teach. The doctrine in question, concerning Jesus, was discounted as false and the author's books were ordered to be burned.

There was discussion at the Council about the problem of different groups of Christians observing Easter (the celebration of Jesus' resurrection) on different days based on various calculations. Constantine thought it would be better to have a consistent date that all could keep together no matter where the Christians lived.[4]

According to the Vornholts, the Council chose to consistently have Easter in the spring on a Sunday, which forced the Jews to lose their luni-solar observance. They feel that locking Easter onto a Sunday forced the observance of Passover to the pagan weekly cycle instead of the lunar cycle. This in turn, they claim, made Sabbath a fixed day on Saturday of the weekly cycle since the Sabbath would need to be the day prior to the resurrection. "The law made it illegal to use the Biblical calendar and it persecuted those who still tried to use it."[5]

A few goals the Vornholts assumed the Council of Nicaea made are:

1. Standardize the planetary week of seven days making dies Solis [Sunday] the first day of the week, with dies Saturni [Saturday] the last day of the week.

2. Guarantee that Passover and Easter would never fall on the same day.

3. Exalt dies Solis as the day of worship for both pagans and Christians.[6]

It has already been shown how a Lunar Sabbath could never have been observed by Jews or Jesus. The continuous weekly cycle has been in existence since Creation and the luni-solar calendar was not needed for feast days after the death of Jesus. We have also seen that history documents that the Jewish Sabbath was already kept on the day known as Saturday.

The truth is the Council of Nicaea only set two rules regarding Easter: 1) keeping it independent from the Jewish luni-solar calendar and 2) worldwide uniformity. No details were specified on how it was to be calculated. This was worked out through the centuries and produced a number of controversies. Though the Council did suggest

Easter should be observed on a Sunday on a lunar month of their own calculations, the Council did not decree that Easter must fall on Sunday. "Nor did the Council decree that Easter must never coincide with Nisan 15 (the first Day of Unleavened Bread, now commonly called 'Passover') in the Hebrew calendar."[7]

Contrary to the view that the Sunday was exalted as the day of worship and the planetary week standardized by making Sunday the first day of the week (rather than Saturday), there is no evidence that this was even discussed at the Council of Nicaea, let alone established. All the changes at the Council that were supposed to force the Jews to give up their "Biblical calendar" did not happen. Neither did any persecuting power occur because of a set law.

SUNDAY EMERGES

The sun god had grown in importance to pagan Rome and was elevated above the other planetary gods. The observance of Sunday (the day after the Sabbath) started out very gradually by the Romans. At the start of the second century some pagan Roman dignitaries started to keep Sunday as a rest day instead of Saturday out of spite for the Jews.

It was at first introduced as a holiday or festival to Gentile Christians and slowly gained popularity over the Sabbath day (which had become solemn and prayerful).[8] This process began in the early part of the second century and culminated in the fourth century.[9]

The Roman Christians chose Sunday as their festival day because it was originally on a Sunday that Jesus arose. The resurrection was a huge victory for Christians and they were not going to forget this important detail. This confirms that Sunday was still considered the same "first day" on which Jesus arose.

Later the Roman emperor forced Sabbath-keepers to spend the Sabbath fasting, rather than the joyful day God had designed. This was difficult for many Christians who already fasted on the Jewish Preparation day, Friday, and now the Sabbath. By Sunday, they were grateful for a day to feast. For many, Sabbath became a dreaded day.

Due to the Jews' repeated revolts against the Romans, an anti-Jewish feeling grew in Rome and the trend was to reject anything Jewish. It became common for even the Roman "Christian" church to cast out "judaizers"— the Christians that still worshiped like the Jews. Many Christians had begun observing Sunday along with their prayer and fasting on the Sabbath. However, anyone who was associated with the Jews in any way was persecuted. Abandoning the Sabbath for Sunday worship gave many the relief from persecution they desired. Many true Sabbath-keeping Christians in Rome went underground to escape or they fled to outlying secluded places where Rome had not penetrated to continue to keep the true Sabbath.

One of these groups, the Waldensian Christians, resisted the power of Rome by fleeing to the wilderness. They could trace their ancestry back to the days when Paul first preached to the faithful Sabbath-keepers in the mountains of Italy. The power on the throne might change the day of worship, but there were always some who obeyed God rather then man.[10] They had been taught to keep Moses' law to the letter and their religion was unspoiled for hundreds of years.

FOURTH CENTURY

Though for a brief moment many nations honored the weekly seventh-day Sabbath in the early centuries AD as God designed, Satan was not satisfied letting it stay that way. He made sure there were enough slight changes through the years to draw people away from God's holy day until he caused men to outright crush God's Sabbath.

Because the emperor, Constantine, had a mother who was Christian, he observed the horrors of persecution as a child. In 313 AD, he granted freedom of worship and equal rights to all religious groups in the empire, in the form of legalizing Christianity, and the persecution stopped. Interestingly, Christians in general became less committed and half-converted pagans entered the Christian world, bringing with them their version of worship.

In 321 AD, Constantine traded the day of Saturn for Sunday as the first day of their week and made a law to make Sunday a rest day. Notice it was *a* rest day, not *the* rest day. Sunday did not legally take the place of Sabbath. While many God-fearing Christians were gradually led to regard Sunday as possessing a degree of sacredness, they still held the true Sabbath as holy to the Lord and observed it in obedience to the fourth commandment.[11] For several more centuries, Sabbath and Sunday were observed side by side.

With the slight change in the Roman cycle, man unknowingly synchronized his cycle with God's. With Sunday being the first day of the Roman cycle and also day one of the Jewish week, no one was without excuse as to when God's holy seventh-day Sabbath was. This weekly cycle, from the influence of the Jews, has since gained almost universal acceptance and practice in the modern world.

SUNDAY WORSHIP REPLACES SABBATH

Only after coming into power in 598 AD did the Roman church attempt to enforce keeping Sunday work-free. They used threat, law, and persecution. Those who defied the church by staying faithful to truth were killed.

It wasn't until the colonies of America were established that the preserved Sabbath was able to come out in the open again. It was brought over by those who had been keeping it in the old world, passed down by their fathers. The colony of Rhode Island was founded by a sincere man, Roger Williams, who allowed Sabbath-keepers to live with him.

Soon after the Roman church lost its power, just before the nineteenth century, the Sabbath torch was again passed on to a group of people totally believing in God's Word. The Seventh-day Adventist church was formed, proclaiming God's Word fully to the world, including His never-forgotten Sabbath day.

> He [Satan] is well pleased when men and women exalt Sunday; for he has been working for centuries to place the first day of the week where the seventh should be.[12]

If Satan is working to transfer the holiness of the seventh day to the first day, and the first day is Sunday, obviously the true seven-day weekly cycle today is still intact. We know even now the day Satan is exalting is still the same—Sunday. Though it took centuries to establish this day over the Sabbath, it is now the acceptable day of worship for Christians all over the world. However, this false day of worship will not prevail in the end, for God's people will be keeping His true commandments and will continue to keep the true Sabbath in heaven.[13]

---

1. Vornholt, eLaine and Vornholt-Jones, Laura Lee. *History of a Lie*, p. 31, emphasis supplied.

2. Vornholt, *The Great Calendar Controversy*, p. 43, emphasis supplied.

3. Ibid., p. 45, emphasis supplied.

4. "First Council of Nicaea," see wikipedia.com

5. Vornholt, *History of a Lie*, p. 27.

6. Ibid., p. 26.

7. "First Council of Nicaea," See wikipedia.com.

8. Voice of Prophecy, *Authoritative Quotations on the Sabbath and Sunday*, p. 30.

9. Pope Sylvester (314-335 AD) stated, "If every Sunday is to be observed joyfully by the Christians on account of the resurrection, then every Sabbath on account of the burial is to be regarded in execration of the Jews.", quoted

by Cardinal S.R.E. Humbert, *Adversus Graecorum Calumias 6*, PL 143, 937 1054 AD.

10. Haskell, Stephen, *Story of Daniel the Prophet*, (N.Y.: Bible Training School, 1999) p. 238.

11. White, Ellen G. *The Great Controversy*, p. 53, emphasis supplied.

12. White, Ellen G., *Review and Herald*, (June 4, 1901) par. 10.

13. Revelation 14:12, Isaiah 66:22,23.

CHAPTER 9

EVIL ORIGINS AND PAGAN THINGS

THE WEEKLY CYCLE FROM BABYLON?

Lunar Sabbatarians claim the weekly cycle originated with the Babylonians who kept an "evil" day every seven days in honor of their god Marduk (supposedly the same name for Saturn). On those evil days, terrible occultic sacrifices were practiced. They consider this a definite reason for Christians not to worship on Saturday. Is there even proof that the day of worshiping Marduk fell on a "Saturday" as we know it, even if Saturn was another name for Marduk?

Claiming that evil was done on Saturdays by Babylonians and others in history does not eliminate God's original command for His holy day. It is not proof that the day didn't coincide with God's true Sabbath just because pagans were worshiping on that day. Satan has counterfeits for almost everything important to God. Did you realize many pagan temples have holy and most holy places set up very similar to the Biblical Sanctuary? What they did there were indescribable evil and occultic practices. Does that mean

God's original design was bad? No, Satan tried to corrupt it, which is possibly even further proof of it being God's special and holy day.

Another example of Satan corrupting God's perfect design is the throne of God. The Bible says the New Jerusalem has the same height as its width and that God's throne is high and lifted up. Does this sound like a pyramid? Possibly. Seeing pyramids all over the world gives us an idea that Satan knew exactly what God's throne looked like. The observances that were performed on those earthly pyramids were extremely occultic, even involving human sacrifices, but that doesn't make God's throne evil, even if that is what Satan used as the basis for the pyramids.[1]

Satan is a master at deceiving the human race into changing the meanings of something God created into something that elevates himself. For instance, he has corrupted God's values in music, sex, family, animals, astronomy, etc. Instead of avoiding these things as "evil," we as Christians should be willing to help restore them back to their beautiful significance.

When the Romans adopted the Jewish weekly cycle they chose different Babylonian gods after which to name their days. But even this does not prove that the weekly cycle came from Babylon.

Yes, we live in a world that uses names that originated in paganism. But using a label to communicate with others in the language they understand does not mean we are worshiping the original deities. In this book any reference to the Sabbath being on Saturday is only due to differentiating the weekly Sabbath from the Lunar Sabbath. Seventh-day Adventists talk about their day of worship as the Sabbath, rather than Saturday, leaving out the pagan name as much as possible, unless communicating with others who would not understand. What is important is that the day we set aside to worship God is the day He originally specified—the Sabbath of the Lord of Creation.

WERE JESUS, THE APOSTLES, AND ELLEN WHITE PAGANS?

In following the Lunar Sabbatarian concept that any word, name, or calendar concept coming from the Babylonians, Romans, or Greeks is defiled for our use, some difficulties arise. We would have to throw out much of our current language and traditions.

The Jews used the biblical language of Hebrew when they were taken to Babylon. The Old Testament was written in Hebrew. However, when they returned from captivity, they were speaking the pagan language of the Babylonians—Aramaic. Horror of horrors, Jesus also spoke Aramaic! Would that make Him a pagan? Of course not! The apostles wrote in Greek! Does that make them pagan? The Jews even adopted the Babylonian names for their months after their exile. There is no record of God reprimanding those practices. Using these words did not conflict with the commandments of God, such as keeping Sunday as Sabbath would, so it does not appear to be offensive to God. With this in mind, is it immoral to call our week days by pagan names?

What about our use of government issued money? Because our money has occultic symbols on it, does that mean we can't use it? No. Jesus and His disciples used Roman (pagan) coins with the depiction of Caesar, who was considered a god. Jesus would have also needed to submit to the Roman civil (Julian) calendar to determine tax time. Regarding matters pertaining to the government in control, Jesus said to respect them. But at the same time, in matters pertaining to God, we are to give Him His due.

In both writing and speaking, Ellen White consistently used the common names of the days of the week— Sunday, Monday, Tuesday, Wednesday, Thursday, Friday, and Saturday. She used them only as labels which are understood by everyone. There was no hint of worshiping pagan gods, nor did God ever give her any reproof for using those names. God never guided His people to avoid their use, as if using them or the common calendar was idolatry. So, is the weekly cycle pagan and the day Saturday evil? Absolutely not.

And how can an orderly calendar be evil if based on astronomical factors? We need to give more credit to those who brought order out of the originally chaotic calendar in the early Roman period. God has ordained governments to keep control in this world, and organizing a civil calendar is something He would approve of, bringing order out of chaos. God recognized our need for keeping track of large amounts of time, which is why He gave us the sun and moon for counting months and years. Men have used these astronomical units for keeping time for thousands of years and have been fairly accurate in their mathematical calculations. We can be thankful that the man-made calendar we use today allows God's week to cycle within its structure.

THE ORIGIN OF THE LUNAR SABBATH THEORY

Every theory has a beginning. Since the Lunar Sabbath could not have come from Creation, where did it come from? Lunar Sabbatarians continually refer to Babylon as the origin for the evil days and weekly cycle we observe today. But in reality, the Lunar Sabbath theory lies closer to Babylonian origins than anything they claim about the weekly cycle and Saturday Sabbath.

In fact, the Babylonians kept a lunar cycle not unlike the Lunar Sabbatarians. Their seven days started at the crescent moon and counted to the 7th, 14th, 21st, and 28th days. They also had extra days before the start of the next crescent moon.[2] Could it be the Lunar Sabbath idea has a pagan origin?

There seems to be more of a feeling of celestial body worship by those who are using the moon to mark their sabbaths than those who are following the weekly cycle of Creation. Lunar Sabbatarians are fixated on everything the moon does. Following moon cycles is eerily like the pagan worship of the moon and the moon gods. Jews only observed the new moons as they pertained to the months God appointed for their feasts. God never intended His people be so consumed with the moon or sun or any other celestial body. Such focus could cause them to worship the creation instead of the Creator.

Early in the twentieth century there was an obsessive amount of research going on by European critical scholars trying to prove that the weekly cycle and Sabbath came from origins other than a Creator God. These scholars are the ones who suggested that the week's origin related to Babylon's "evil days" and they developed the Sabbath from the phases of the moon. Even though the idea was disproved and abandoned many years later,[3] it evidently continues to grow through the Lunar Sabbath theory today.

---

1. Maniscalco, Joe, "The Mystery of the Pyramids," *Mysteries Unmasked*. 2. Kurlinski, John. "'In The Beginning' and other References to Time." (Presented to University of Iowa, 2007).

3. Rodriguez, Angel. "What About a Lunar Sabbath," *Adventist World*, see adventistworld.org/article.

CHAPTER 10

COMMENCING THE SABBATH

SUNSET TO SUNSET OR SUNRISE TO SUNRISE

An intriguing part of the Lunar Sabbath theory is the belief that the Biblical day begins and ends at sunrise rather than sunset, as the Jews and Seventh-day Adventists believe. This concept not only affects keeping or breaking the sacred hours of the Sabbath, but also affects whether Jesus could have been crucified on Friday in 31 AD, as covered in the following chapter.

Lunar Sabbatarians base the concept of the day beginning at sunrise on the text referring to the morning of the resurrection, "Now after the Sabbath, as the first day of the week began to dawn, Mary Magdalene and the other Mary came to see the tomb."[1]

Referring to the crucifixion, the Vornholts say because Joseph of Arimathea waited until evening to begin the process of seeking permission to have possession of Jesus' body, they couldn't have been ready for the Sabbath if the

Sabbath hours began at sundown. Taking Jesus' body down from the cross, cleaning and wrapping it, etc., would have taken them into the night hours to do their work and they would not have finished until it started to grow light.[2] They claim that the evening hours begin around 3:00PM and last until sunset. Since Jesus died at 3:00PM[3], the time of the evening sacrifice, there supposedly was not enough time before an evening Sabbath would have begun.

In reality, Jerusalem was not a very big city and it would not have taken Joseph long to return from getting permission from Pilate for Jesus' body. According to the *Starry Night*[4] software, sundown in Jerusalem on Passover Friday in 31 AD would have been at 9:14PM. Jesus died at 3:00PM, which gave several hours to get the basics done and be home before the Sabbath began at sunset.

If Sabbath had not started until the next day's sunrise, there would have been more than 14 hours for the disciples to take Jesus down from the cross, wrap His body, and lay it in a "nearby" tomb. If they had worked all night, it seems it would have been completed, contrary to what the Bible says. The disciples didn't have time to finish this work and had to go back on Sunday morning to complete the preparation of Jesus body.[5]

An interesting tidbit on this topic comes from the biography of Ellen White. The context mentions the issue of some people keeping the Sabbath starting at sunrise and God giving her a vision to correct that error.

In the State of Maine in 1847–1848, some took the position

that the Sabbath commenced at sunrise, quoting as support, Matthew 28:1: "In the end of the sabbath, as it began to dawn toward the first day of the week" (see RH, Feb. 25, 1868). A vision given to Ellen White checked this error in principle, for the angel repeated the words of the scripture "From even unto even, shall ye celebrate your sabbath."[6]

BIBLICAL EVIDENCE FOR
SUNSET RECKONING

The Bible is clear that the Sabbath begins at sunset and extensive documentation shows that the Jews have kept the Sabbath beginning at sundown through the ages and throughout the world. For example, in a story in the gospel of Mark, the people of Capernaum didn't bring their sick to be healed by Jesus on Sabbath until after sundown.

> Then they went into Capernaum, and immediately on the Sabbath He entered the synagogue and taught. At evening, when the sun had set, they brought to Him all who were sick and those who were demon-possessed.[7]

Jesus did heal on the Sabbath though. In fact, He had healed a man in the synagogue that morning and also Peter's mother-in-law when they got to his home. But the people respected the Sabbath and feared the wrath of the religious leaders. Not wanting to break the Sabbath, they waited until it was over at sundown to bring all of the sick to Him to be healed.

Samuele Bacchiocchi deals with this topic quite extensively in his book *The Time of the Crucifixion and the*

Resurrection. There is too much information to include here, but he agrees that there were biblical writers who talked about days both as starting at sunset and starting at sunrise. After giving a number of scriptural examples that could indicate sunrise reckoning, he says, "We have found that the indications for the sunset reckoning are more abundant and explicit than those for the sunrise reckoning. We have suggested that the choice of one method over the other could have been influenced by whether the events being reported occurred during the day or during the night."[8]

Dr. Bacchiocchi's ending conclusion after extensive study between sunrise or sunset reckoning is that the evidence of scripture and the Jewish culture have pointed to sunset as the method in determining the beginning of the Sabbath. "All the passages in the Old and New Testament which refer to the time element of Sabbath-keeping clearly suggest a sunset reckoning."[9]

While we do not base our fundamental beliefs on tradition, the fact is that Jews have had the tradition of Sabbath beginning at Friday sunset for thousands of years. Speaking of tradition, I have witnessed a sample Passover that a typical family would have celebrated and the details that are incorporated are amazing. How can the Jews remember these details so perfectly for thousands of years? Partly because the traditions have been recorded, kept every year, and carefully passed down through all their generations. Traditions are important to them. How could they have forgotten or changed something as important as starting the Sabbath at Friday sunset instead of at Sabbath morning sunrise?

I emailed a conservative Jew and asked him about the keeping of the Sabbath. He confirmed the Sabbath always has a set time in the weekly cycle and it starts every Friday night at sunset.[10] The Jews could not have gotten this from the Romans. The Romans never had traditions of lighting candles and saying specific evening prayers to welcome in a holy day.

ELLEN WHITE AND SUNSET RECKONING

The Vornholts admit that Ellen White thought Sabbath began at sundown, but say that she just didn't understand the truth of a sunrise to sunrise Sabbath during her time, kind of like Daniel didn't understand his 2300 day prophetic vision.

> Did Ellen White believe the Sabbath was to be kept from sunset Friday to sunset Saturday? Yes. Does that in any way affect her standing as a prophet of the Lord? Absolutely not. Ellen White must not be held to an unfair standard. Daniel has never been denounced as a false prophet simply because he did not understand everything.[11]

However, there is a big difference between Daniel's prophetic vision and Ellen White's visions, such as when she was clearly shown the events surrounding Christ's crucifixion. The vision given to Daniel involved symbols and times for which he had no understanding to their meanings, other than that God had set a limited amount of time for His people as a nation to accept or reject Him. Through vision, Ellen White witnessed actual past events as they occurred. There were no symbols or time prophecies, only a depiction of what took place.

"In 1889 she told of how 'the betrayal, trial, and crucifixion of Jesus' had passed before her *point by point* (Letter 14, 1889)." In 1900 she wrote: *"Heavenly scenes were presented to me in the life of Christ,* pleasant to contemplate, and again painful scenes which were not always pleasant for Him to bear which pained my heart."[12]

Ellen White, through vision, was an eyewitness to these events and should have been able to see what part of day it was when she was in vision. Seventh-day Adventists believe God gave her accurate views of what happened, and that we can take her word seriously. She never said she didn't understand the scenes of the cross or when the Sabbath begins.

The Spirit of Prophecy is so clear on the time of day when the Sabbath began that it seems impossible to twist the meanings of the following quotes:

> At last Jesus was at rest. The long day of shame and torture was ended. *As the last rays of the setting sun ushered in the Sabbath,* the Son of God lay in quietude in Joseph's tomb. His work completed, His hands folded in peace, He rested through the sacred hours of the Sabbath day.[13]

> *The Sabbath was now drawing on,* and it would be a violation of its sanctity for the bodies to hang upon the cross. So, using this as a pretext, the leading Jews requested Pilate that the death of the victims might be hastened, and their bodies be removed

before the setting of the sun.[14]

The women were last at the cross, and last at the tomb of Christ. *While the evening shades were gathering,* Mary Magdalene and the other Marys lingered about the resting place of their Lord, shedding tears of sorrow over the fate of Him whom they loved. "And they returned, . . . and rested the Sabbath day according to the commandment." Luke 23:56…*At the setting of the sun on the evening of the preparation day the trumpets sounded, signifying that the Sabbath had begun.*[15]

CONFUSION ABOUT THE SABBATH STARTING AT 6:00 PM

The Vornholts' criticism of the Sabbath beginning at sundown is based on the fact that for almost 10 years "early Adventists" believed in keeping the Sabbath from 6:00PM on Friday to 6:00PM on Saturday. When they studied into the real meaning of "even to even" in 1855 and realized it might be at the setting of the sun, an angel appeared to Ellen White and confirmed that Sabbath really began at sundown.

I saw that it is even so: "From even unto even, shall ye celebrate your Sabbath." Said the angel: "Take the word of God, read it, *understand, and ye cannot err.* Read carefully, and ye shall there find what even is, and when it is." I asked the angel if the frown of God had been upon His people for commencing the Sabbath as they had. I was directed back to the first rise of the Sabbath, and followed the people of God up to this time, but did not see that the Lord was displeased, or frowned upon them. I inquired why it had been thus, that at this late day we must change the time of commencing the Sabbath. Said the angel: *"Ye shall understand, but not yet, not yet."* Said the angel: "If light comes, and that light is set aside or rejected, then comes condemnation and the frown of God; but before the light comes, there is no sin, for there is no light for them to reject." I saw that it was in the minds of some that the Lord had shown that the Sabbath commenced at six o'clock, when I had only seen that it commenced at "even," and it was inferred that even was at six. I saw that the servants of God must draw together, press together.[16]

The Vornholts claim this vision shows that Ellen White did not understand when the Sabbath was truly to commence and that someday they would realize it began at sunrise. But what Ellen White did not understand was why they hadn't already known the truth that the Sabbath began at sunset and had been observing it incorrectly for almost a decade. The angel promised her that she *would understand and not err* on this point. She lived and taught this point for 60 years after this vision, and never changed her view that the Sabbath began at sundown on Friday evening.

---

1. Matthew 28:1.

2. Vornholt, eLaine and Vornholt-Jones, Laura Lee. *The Great Calendar Controversy* (Colbert, WA: 4 Angels Publications), p. 21.

3. Matthew 27: 46.

4. *Starry Night,* computer software (Imaginova Corp., 2006).

5. Mark 16:1–2.

6. White, Arthur. *Ellen G. White: The Early Years,* Vol. 1, (Hagerstown, MD: Review & Herald Pub., 1985) p. 322.

7. Mark 1:21, 32.

8. Bacchiocchi, Samuele. *The Time of the Crucifixion and the Resurrection,* (Michigan: Biblical Perspectives, 1985, ed.) p. 87.

9. Ibid, p. 108.

10. Lord, Jonathon. Answer to email question (American-Israeli Cooperative

Enterprise, March 27, 2009).

11. Vornholt, loc. cit., p. 22.

12. White, Arthur. *Ellen G. White, Volume 3, The Lonely Years, 1876–1891,* p. 93, emphasis supplied. Review & Herald (1984), Washington D.C.

13. White, Ellen G. *The Desire of Ages,* p. 769, emphasis supplied.

14. Ibid, p. 771, emphasis supplied.

15. Ibid., p. 774, emphasis supplied.

16. White, Ellen G. *Testimonies for the Church,* Vol. 1, p. 116, emphasis supplied.

CHAPTER 11

THE 31 AD QUESTION

CRUCIFIXION ON FRIDAY IN 31 AD

Christians all over the world believe Jesus was crucified on a Friday. Seventh-day Adventists, more specifically through Bible prophecy, determine the year 31 AD as Jesus' death. But the Vornholts and other Lunar Sabbatarians challenge that Jesus could not have died on a Friday in the year 31 AD. They say,

> "Babylon, that huge monolith of mystery, intrigue, deception and paganism, is precariously balanced on one little lie: that Christ was crucified on a Friday and resurrected on a Sunday."[1]

Seventh-day Adventists, using the 70-week prophecy of Daniel 9 which started in 457 BC, calculate the time of the Messiah's appearing to begin in 27 AD. The Messiah being cut off in the midst of the week results in Jesus being crucified in the spring of 31 AD. The question for Seventh-day Adventists isn't so much the year, because there is good evidence for that. The question is how could Jesus have been crucified on a Friday when the evidence seems to indicate otherwise.

There are many records surrounding the events of Jesus' death. If we look into these, we can begin to reconstruct the crucifixion week and find out if there is any discrepancy with the weekly cycle. What do we know for sure about this week?

1. Jesus' crucifixion was during Passover week.[2]

2. Passover in 31 AD fell in April.[3]

3. Passover was the 14th day from the sighting of the crescent moon and should be near a full moon.[4]

4. Jesus was crucified and died on the Preparation Day, which is the day before the Jewish Sabbath.[5]

5. He was three days and three nights in the "heart of the earth."[6]

6. Jesus lay in the tomb over the seventh-day Sabbath.[7]

7. He rose early the first day of the week.[8]

THE LAST WEEK OF CHRIST

In her book *The Desire of Ages*, Ellen White describes with amazing details the week leading up to Jesus' crucifixion. She starts with Jesus arriving at his friend Lazarus' house in Bethany, six days before the Passover.

> The Savior had reached Bethany only six days before the Passover, and according to His custom had sought rest at the home of Lazarus. The crowds of travelers who passed on to the city spread the tidings that He was on His way to Jerusalem, and that He would rest over the Sabbath at Bethany.[9]

According to Strong's Concordance and what we have already discussed, the Jewish day was from sunset to sunset. So what day was it that Jesus arrived in Bethany? Because He stayed over for the Sabbath and left on the first day of the week for Jerusalem, He likely arrived just before sunset on Friday evening. The day was already gone, so sunset Sabbath started day 1. Let's start counting by the chart below (the slanted lines indicate the sunsets beginning the following days):

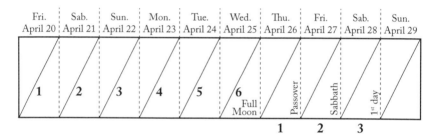

Ellen White clearly states that the day Jesus died was a Friday, a parallel of the Friday when the Godhead finished the work of Creation.

It was in God's plan that the work which Christ had engaged to do should be completed on a Friday, and that on the Sabbath He should rest in the tomb, even as the Father and Son had rested after completing Their creative work.[10]

The Savior was buried on Friday, the sixth day of the week. The women prepared spices and ointments with which to embalm their Lord, and laid them aside, until the Sabbath was past. Not even the work of embalming the body of Jesus would they do upon the Sabbath day.[11]

CONFLICTS WITH THE FULL MOON?

Lunar Sabbatarians argue that Passover always falls exactly on the day of the full moon. The United States Naval Observatory (USNO) places the 100% full moon in April of 31 AD on Wednesday, April 25.

This is hard evidence to Lunar Sabbatarians that the Jews could not have been using the Julian weekly calendar, because they say there is no way Passover, the crucifixion, and Sabbath could line up with the Friday and Saturday of the Julian calendar. They show that it does work with a Lunar calendar.

So how can we explain Jesus being crucified on a Friday? Remember, as discussed previously, in ancient times the new moon was always decided by observation. This means if the new moon was not seen right away, the start of the month and the feast day would be delayed. The reality in using observation was that the crescent moon sometimes was not sighted up to four days from the calculated new moon.[12]

If the "observed" crescent moon was just one day later than the USNO's calculated date, and a day begins at sundown as described in the previous chapter, then the Passover would have started on what we now call Thursday evening (instead of Wednesday). This would have been the first part of Friday using the biblical sundown principle.

The diagram on the next page may help clarify this.[13]

However, according to Ellen White in *The Desire of Ages,*

1st Day Sunday	2nd Day Monday	3rd Day Tuesday	4th Day Wednesday	5th Day Thursday	Preparation Friday	Sabbath Sabbath
8	9	10 *New Moon ●	11	12	13 Crescent of New Moon Observed? ☾	14
15 N 2	16 N 3	17 N 4	18 N 5	19 N 6	20 N 7	21 N 8
22 N 9	23 N 10	24 N 11	25 *Full Moon ○ N 12	26 N 13	27 ✝ N 14 Lamb Slain	28 Passover Lamb Eaten N 15
29 Sheaf waved N 16						
First day after Passover Sabbath *JESUS RESURRECTED*			Last Supper/ Gethsemane		Passover Day *JESUS CRUCIFIED*	Passover Sabbath *FIRST DAY OF UNLEAVENED BREAD*

*Official dates for New and Full Moons as given by the US Naval Observatory

N 1 = Nissan 1, N 2 = Nissan 2, etc.

In the diagram, the shaded area of each day is the night portion (the first part of the day) which begins at the setting of the sun. Midnight (dotted line) is in the middle of the shaded areas, which is how we define days in our modern culture.

the Passover moon was "broad and full" that Thursday night Jesus prayed in the garden.[14] How can that be, if the full moon was on Wednesday night? Scientifically, the moon can be considered broad and full for around 72 hours—the night before and the night after the official day of the full moon. Thursday night was well within the 72 hours, since it was the night after the 100% certified USNO full moon.

So is it possible for Christ to have died on a Friday with the full moon occurring on a Wednesday? "The answer is, yes, a Friday crucifixion in 31 AD is entirely 'possible' according to astronomical calculations (for whatever they may be worth), granted a few unprovable, yet reasonable assumptions." If the sighting of the crescent moon was even just one day off, it is feasible to assume Passover fell accurately... on Friday, April 27, 31 AD.[15]

EXPERT TESTIMONY ON LUNAR CALCULATION

Francis D. Nichol, editor of the Seventh-day Adventist Bible Commentary, wrote to several leading astronomers "asking their opinion 1) concerning the degree of accuracy possible in reckoning back to the Julian date of any new moon or full moon in Christ's time on the basis of modern lunar tables; and 2) concerning the elements of uncertainty in converting such an ancient date from astronomical terms to a specific day in the Jewish calendar, as would be necessary in order to assign a Julian date to the crucifixion."[16]

The astronomers were from various locations around the world but they all agreed that although it is possible to calculate the new moon to a close margin in 31 AD, it is impossible to determine when the Jews may have started counting the month of Nissan, leading up to the Passover. Here are a few statements from the letters from these experts. The first one is from the USNO (the pivotal authority for the Lunar Sabbatarian view that the full moon was on Wednsday night, thus disallowing a Friday crucifixion[17]).

> The interval from new moon to the appearance of the crescent cannot be calculated from theory alone....the fact remains that purely local conditions can invalidate even the most careful work in respect of a particular observation of the lunar crescent.... The dates of Nissan 14 in the years of the first century of the Christian era cannot possibly be determined by any astronomical calculation; they can be fixed, if by any means at all, only by the study and interpretation of contemporary records. - G. M. Clemence, Director, Nautical Almanac, U.S. Naval Observatory

> If one assumes, for once, that the beginning of the month was based on the observation of the new crescent, one cannot affirm nor deny with complete certainty that a computed determination of a 14 Nissan would coincide with that obtained from actual observations of the new crescent. - Dr. Ulrich Baehr

> I cannot answer authoritatively your second question, since this depends upon the theoretical estimate for the interval between new Moon and the first observation of the visible lunar crescent....but the fact remains that purely local conditions can invalidate even the most careful work in respect of a particular observation of the lunar crescent.- D. H. Sadler

> All modern tables have to make arbitrary assumptions as to

the visibility conditions in antiquity in general or in specific localities. These assumptions are highly arbitrary, and even for modern times, extremely unreliable. Since the phenomenon of first visibility is connected with sunset, all such tables involve inaccuracies of one full day.... - O. Neugebauer[18]

Astronomy shows it is impossible for us who live two millennia distant from the actual events to disprove the Friday crucifixion based on purely astronomical evidence of when the new and full moons were calculated to have taken place. The unknown factors of the culture and observation mean we cannot know for certain from our vantage point in history—unless we take historical writings and/or the Spirit of Prophecy as authoritative. They both place the crucifixion on Friday.

Documentation of the 1938 Seventh-day Adventist General Conference Research Committee shows they did an exhaustive study into Jewish dating methods which included the 31 AD issue. They studied the moon and the other factors and came to the conclusion that:

Friday, April 27, 31 AD, Julian time, has been demonstrated to be the only date during the public ministry of Christ which satisfies 1) the Bible requirement for a Friday Passover crucifixion and 2) the definite demands of astronomy for the corresponding coincident positions of sun, moon, and earth.[19]

THREE DAYS AND THREE NIGHTS

There is also debate over the day when Jesus was actually crucified based on His saying He would be "three days and three nights in the heart of the earth."[20] Many have built a Wednesday or Thursday crucifixion theory because of this statement. But did Jesus mean a literal 72 hours like we count three days and three nights today?

A well-known Seventh-day Adventist pastor, Doug Batchelor, explains that "the heart of the earth" actually refers to being in the clutches of Satan, not necessarily in the tomb. This would have started on Thursday night when Jesus began suffering the separation from the Father in the Garden of Gethsemane. That is when He started to drink the cup of God's wrath, thus involving three nights: Thursday, Friday, and Saturday, as well as parts of three days: Friday, Sabbath, Sunday.[21]

Another way of looking at this issue is given in the Seventh-Day Adventist Bible Commentary. Jesus mentioned the same period of three days, the time between His death and resurrection, in a few different places. While they may mean different times to us, to the ancients of His day, they meant the same thing. At various times He stated "after three days" (Mark 8:31), on "the third day" (Matthew 16:21; 17:23; 20:19; 27:64), "in three days" (Matthew 26:61; 27:40, Mark 14:58, John 2:19–21), and "three days and three nights" (Matthew 12:40). So, did Jesus contradict Himself by giving different literal time frames? No. Even the priests and Pharisees understood what He meant. They asked Pilate to have the tomb guarded "until the third day." Obviously, "after three days" to the Jews meant "the third day."

The problem with modern thinking is defining biblical terms based on our current mathematical mind set and understanding. We incorrectly take what we think something means and apply it to a culture that existed in a different part of the world 2000 years ago. In reality, the ancient method of reckoning was inclusive. They counted differently than we do.

When a baby is born, we say he is 0 years old. That baby would have had to live for twelve full months before we would say he is 1 year old. For the whole second year of its life, we would say he was 1 year old. In the ancients' mind, when a child is born, it is year 1. When it reaches the second year—at his first birthday—he is in year 2. The Bible demonstrates this with Noah. He was literally "a son of 600 years" "in the six hundredth year" of his life.[22] The same reasoning can be applied to our centuries. The first century included all the years from 1 to 100, after that it became the second century. When we lived in the 20th century we were still only in the 1900s and since the year 2000 we are in the 21st century.

In the Jewish method, inclusive counting included the day (or year) it started counting from, no matter how small a fraction the beginning or ending day (or year) was. Applying this to Jesus' statements, we can be sure His hearers counted the three days as:

1. The day of the crucifixion.

2. The day after that event.

3. The "third" day after (by modern count, the second day after).[23]

So if Jesus' prophecy of being in the heart of the earth three days started Thursday night, when was it fulfilled? The Bible says it was the first day of the week. Later on that same day, two disciples were on the road to Emmaus when Jesus joined them. They talked of their disappointment in the crucifixion of Jesus. Jesus answered, "Today is the third day since these things were done."[24] They should have remembered His prophecy and known He was to be raised by this day. Sunday, the day after the Sabbath, was obviously the third day.

Using Jewish methods of calculating the new moons and counting days, there should be no question that Jesus was crucified on a Friday and resurrected on a Sunday.

1. Vornholt, eLaine and Vornholt-Jones, Laura Lee. *The Great Calendar Controversy* (Colbert, WA: 4 Angels Publications), p. 67.

2. Mark 14:14–15.

3. White, James. *Bible Adventism*, (Battle Creek, MI: SDA Publishing Assoc.., 1972) p. 143.

4. White, Ellen G. *The Desire of Ages*, p. 685.

5. Mark 15:42.

6. Matthew 12:40.

7. Mark 16:1.

8. Mark 16:2.

9. White, loc. cit., p. 557.

10. White, Ellen G. *The Man of Sorrows*, (February 24, 1898) pp. 3, 4, emphasis supplied.

11. White, Ellen G. *The Story of Jesus*, p. 157, emphasis supplied.

12. Maxwell, Mervyn. *The Message of Daniel – God Cares*, Volume One, (Boise, ID: Pacific Press Pub. 1981) p. 259.

13. Ibid., p. 263.

14. White, *The Desire of Ages*, p. 685.

15. Maxwell, loc. cit., p. 263.

16. Nichol, F. D. *The Seventh-day Adventist Bible Commentary*, Volume 5, (Review & Herald Publishing Association, 1978).

17. Vornholt, loc. cit., p. 37.

18. Nichol, loc. cit.

19. 1938 Research Committee Report, Part V, p. 52.

20. Matthew 12:40.

21. Batchelor, Doug. *A New Revelation*, (Sacramento, CA: Mountain Ministry, 1993).

22. Genesis 7:6–11.

23. Nichol, loc. cit., Volume 5.

24. Luke 24:21.

CHAPTER 12

LUNAR SABBATH IN PROPHECY?

THE ABOMINATION OF DESOLATION

It is hard to approach the subject of prophecy without getting somewhat theologically technical because it involves prophetic terms even the average Seventh-day Adventist struggles with. And yet *The Great Calendar Controversy* embraces this subject and claims that the change away from the Lunar Sabbath to a weekly cycle is prophesied about in the Bible. So we'll take a brief look at a few of these issues.

It would stand to reason that something as big as *a complete change of calendars aimed at deceiving God's people should be in the Bible.* It is. Amazingly, it's been there the whole time. A diligent study, consistently applying the principles of Biblical interpretation will reveal what has been hidden from casual study. *Jesus Himself referred to this calendar change—both when it occurred under the rising influence of the papacy and when it will be done again in this last generation.*

Matthew 24:15, 16 – "When ye therefore shall see the abomination of desolation, spoken of by Daniel the prophet, stand in the holy place, (whoso readeth let him understand:)

then let them which be in Judea flee into the mountains."[1]

By referring back to the prophecies of Daniel, Christ has shed a floodlight on the true significance of the abomination of desolation and how that will appear disguised as a calendar change law.[2]

Jesus said that the "abomination of desolation" is a calendar change law? Seventh-day Adventists agree that Jesus was giving a dual prophecy, speaking of the soon approaching Roman siege as well as a critical situation at the end of time. However, the application is to the enforced observance of Sunday as the Sabbath of the Lord.

Looking back at the prediction Jesus made about the abomination of desolation, Luke adds a little more detail than the Matthew 24 account, noting that when Jerusalem is surrounded, desolation is near.

But when you see Jerusalem surrounded by armies, then know that its desolation is near. Then let those who are in Judea flee to the mountains, let those who are in the midst of her depart, and let not those who are in the country enter her.[3]

This can be better understood by taking a brief look at history when the Romans attacked Jerusalem in 66 AD and 70 AD.

It turns out that there was an area outside the walls of Jerusalem which was designated as "Holy ground" or a "Holy place." Notice this statement, "When the idolatrous standards of the Romans should be set up in the holy ground, which extended some furlongs outside the city walls, then the followers of Christ were to find safety in flight." *Great Controversy*, p. 26. Notice… it was merely standing as a threat of impending destruction.[4]

Ellen White said, "As the siege of Jerusalem by the Roman armies was the signal for flight to the Judean Christians, so the assumption of power on the part of our nation, in the decree enforcing the papal sabbath, will be a warning to us."[5]*

The Papacy has made known that she sees as her standard of authority: Sunday observance. "Sunday is our mark of authority... The Church is above the Bible, and this transference of Sabbath observance is proof of that fact."[6]

In end-time prophecy, the meaning of the "abomination of desolation" is the posting of Rome's standard, Sunday, the false sabbath. It is not a calendar change.

THE DAILY SACRIFICES TAKEN AWAY

The Great Calendar Controversy again takes us back to Daniel to show how the overthrow of the Lunar Sabbath by the pagan weekly cycle could have been foretold. They start with Daniel 8:11.

> He (the little horn) even exalted himself as high as the Prince of the host; and by him the daily sacrifices were taken away, and the place of His sanctuary was cast down.[7]

Biblical scholars interpret this to mean the little horn (which has been identified as the Roman papacy) tried to make himself as powerful as Christ and he took away the ministry of Christ (which is in the heavenly sanctuary) and cast it down by substituting a false institution of worship–masses and confessionals.

There has been a lot of debate about the exact meaning of "the daily" of Daniel 8:11 and there are two main views about it in Adventism. Very simple descriptions of these views are:

1. The daily sacrifice was taken away and in its place, the papacy has substituted a daily false system of worship, mass, confessionals, etc.

2. The daily was paganism, which was taken away in order to give rise of the papacy.

We're not going to try to resolve that issue. Even Ellen White stated that this is not a "salvation issue."

> It has been presented to me that this is not a subject of vital importance. I am instructed that our brethren are making a mistake in magnifying the importance of the difference in the views that are held. I cannot consent that any of my writings shall be taken as settling this matter. The true meaning of "the daily" is not to be made a test question.[8]

But *The Great Calendar Controversy* states that the Seventh-day Adventist view of Daniel 8:11 is the understanding of only superficial reading. The author's "deeper" meaning of "the daily" means a pagan continual cycle of weeks. They say:

> When these correct definitions are inserted, the rendering of Daniel 8:11 is far different from what a surface reading suggests:

> "The little horn (papacy) magnified and exalted himself even to Jesus Christ and by him (the Little Horn) the *continuous* was presumptuously exalted. The result was that the place of *his (the papacy's) sanctuary* was made *safe and secure.*"

This is the most accurate interpretation of Daniel 8:11. The "continuous," or "continual" (which is the literal translation of the word "daily"), refers to the continuous weekly cycle of the pagan solar calendar. "Daily" is also defined as "continuously without interruption." *This is a perfect description of the continuous, unending cycle of weeks of the pagan Julian and papal Gregorian calendars.*[9]

There are three main differences in the view of Daniel 8:11 between Seventh-day Adventist theology and the Vornholt's theory. They say that after exalting himself, the little horn power 1) exalts the continuous cycle of weeks (instead of the daily sacrifice) so that 2) the little horn power's sanctuary (instead of God's sanctuary) would 3) be made safe and secure (instead of cast down). This interpretation gives a vastly different meaning of Daniel 8:11.

The Vornholts' study took them to their Interlinear Bible to look up the Hebrew words for the verse. When researching the meaning of the words "was cast down" they noticed that the margin gave an optional Hebrew word *shalam* (*Strong's* #7999) meaning "to be safe and secure." However, the Hebrew dictionary shows the original word for "was cast down" was the word *shalak* (Strong's #7993) literally meaning "to cast down," not *shalam*—an entirely opposite meaning![10]

It seems that when deciding the correct meaning between two words with opposite meanings, it would be safest and most honest to take the word which is actually used in the scriptures, not one proposed by an unknown scholar in the margin of a book.

Early Seventh-day Adventist pioneers and scholars were right about the original meaning. This verse is focused on Christ and His ministry being cast down by the changes of papal Rome, not about a calendar change. Once again the Scriptural proof for a Lunar Sabbath has been "cast down."

DUAL APPLICATION?

Another prophetic verse *The Great Calendar Controversy* utilizes is Daniel 9:27. It says:

> Then he shall confirm a covenant with many for one week; But in the middle of the week he shall bring an end to sacrifice and offering. And on the wing of abominations shall be one who makes desolate, even until the consummation, which is determined, is poured out on the desolate.[11]

This is an awesome prophecy about the Messiah and the wonderful sacrifice He made to save us. It looks complicated, but with definitions added according to the context of Daniel 9, this is what Seventh-day Adventists believe the verse means:

> Then he *[Christ]* shall confirm *[confirm]* a covenant *[compact]* with many *[His people]* for one week *[AD 27–34 in time prophecy; God gives the Jewish nation a probation period to decide to follow Christ the Messiah or not]* But in the middle of the week *[AD 31— Christ's death]* He shall bring an end to sacrifice and offering *[the sacrificial system and all its ceremonies]*. And on the wing *[the edge of this time prophecy]* of abominations *[idolatrous Jewish nation]* shall be one who makes desolate *[the Jewish nation brought upon themselves the destruction of Jerusalem and the Temple]*, even until the consumation *[the end]*, which is determined, is poured out

on the desolate *[those that destroyed Jerusalem and the Temple—Rome].*"[12]

While the Vornholts admit that the main meaning of Daniel 9:27 refers to the Messiah, they say there is a dual application that refers to the continuous weekly cycles. They give their rendition as follows:

> When these deeper meanings are understood, Daniel 9:27 reads: "And he shall be strong and prevail. He shall act insolently against the covenant with many for one week. In the midst of the week, he shall cause the sacrifice and the oblation to cease and he shall super-impose his idol sabbath on top of the true Sabbath of the fourth commandment."[13]

A solemn prophecy about the awesome mission of the Messiah can also be speaking about Satan and calendar changes? Is this really an honest interpretation?

There is nothing remotely connected to a pagan calendar change in their text. Their explanation of this verse does not fit the context of Daniel 9 and it is not reasonable to pick a verse out of its context and apply a different meaning to it.

We must be careful in how we interpret the Scriptures. We are not to add or subtract anything from it. A question of validity can certainly be expressed about any theory when there is evidence of misinterpreted Scriptures.

1. Vornholt, eLaine and Vornholt-Jones, Laura Lee. *The Great Calendar Controversy* (Colbert, WA: 4 Angels Publications), p. 52, emphasis supplied.
2. Vornholt, loc. cit., p. 54, emphasis supplied.
3. Luke 21:20–21.
4. Westbrook, David. *Out of the Cities,* (Dave Westbrook, 2001) p. 3, 4.

5. White, Ellen G. *Testimonies for the Church*, vol. 5, p. 464. *The Sunday laws in the last days are to be a signal for Christians to flee to the country, away from the cities, just as the Christians during the attack on Jerusalem.

6. *Catholic Record*, (Sept. 1, 1923).

7. Daniel 8:11.

8. White, Ellen G. *1 Selected Messages*, p. 164.

9. Vornholt, loc. cit., p. 57, emphasis supplied.

10. Mellor, Barry. "Shifting Sand," (Spring City, TN, Seventh Day Wilderness Fellowship).

11. Daniel 9:27.

12. Daniel 9:27, emphasis supplied.

13. Vornholt, loc. cit., p. 62.

CHAPTER 13

PROBLEMS WITH SOURCES

RESEARCH SOURCES

When doing research, such as for this book, it is very important for the author to try to use authoritative sources and to use them properly. That is the only way to come out with valid results which can be trusted.

In studying the Lunar Sabbath view presented by the Vornholts in their books, articles, and websites, it is obvious that they did extensive research. Many of the studies on the change of the Jewish calendar appear at first to be quite valid. However, when they make changes to sources to support their theory, questions arise.

In this chapter, we are going to look at some of the main sources the Vornholts use to support the Lunar Sabbath idea to see if they are valid as quoted.

THE EARTH IS FLAT?

Would it be appropriate to quote a person as saying that

the world is flat, when throughout their writings they state over and over that the world is round and give voluminous evidence to show that? Would that not be misusing their work in some way?

In the Vornholts' books and articles the late Robert L. Odom's writings have been quoted multiple times. Odom's book *Sunday in Roman Paganism* is an excellent resource for the history of the weekly cycle and much of the time their use of his material is very instructional.

But, if you read Odom's book carefully, his statements consistently oppose the teachings of the Vornholts. Yet, they select things he said and use them to support the Lunar Sabbath theory, which is far from anything he ever promoted or wrote.

For example, he clearly defined what he meant by the terms "pagan planetary week" and "biblical week." His definition of the biblical week is the days numbered by Creation with the seventh day as the Sabbath falling on the weekly Saturday. With the pagan planetary week, he shows the days were named for planetary gods and used in pagan worship. Though these weeks ran side-by-side with the Jewish week, he says they were used very differently.

The Vornholts use Robert Odom's statements of the "biblical week" to mean the week according to the Lunar Sabbath theory. They take his words to support the "biblical week which depended upon the moon." Here is one example of their use of his work in a way totally different than how he defined the biblical week, even emphasizing his word

THE LUNAR SABBATH CONSPIRACY

"Biblical" as they quote.

> Biblical calendation was supplanted by pagan solar calendation, and the planetary week replaced the Biblical week which depended upon the moon. "Just as the true Sabbath is inseparably linked with the *Biblical* week, so the false Sabbath of pagan origin needed a weekly cycle. Thus we have found that the planetary week of paganism is Sunday's twin sister, and that the two counterfeit institutions were linked together . . . ." (quoted from Robert Odom, *Sunday in Roman Paganism,* p. 243–244, their emphasis supplied)[1]

Robert Odom wrote a number of books, many regarding the true Sabbath, and was a firm believer in the continuous weekly cycle and the seventh-day Sabbath being on Saturday. The twisting of the original meaning of the source into something that Mr. Odom did not believe or ever intend to write leads one to question how other sources may have been used.

USE OF CATHOLIC SOURCES

In *The Great Controversy,* Ellen White quotes the Catholic church's catechism as part of her evidence that the papacy changed the holiness of the Sabbath from Saturday to Sunday.

> Roman Catholics acknowledge that the change of the Sabbath was made by their church, and declare that Protestants by observing the Sunday are recognizing her power. In the Catholic Catechism of Christian Religion, in answer to a question as to the day to be observed in obedience to the fourth commandment, this statement is made: "During the old law, Saturday was the

day sanctified; but the church, instructed by Jesus Christ, and directed by the Spirit of God, *has substituted Sunday for Saturday;* so now we sanctify the first, not the seventh day. Sunday means, and now is, the day of the Lord.[2]

How do we know which Catholic historians or theologians are trustworthy of being quoted on historical details? Is it valid to use their literature as evidence of the change of the Sabbath from Saturday to Sunday? The Vornholts believe Catholic sources are not reliable because they affirm Saturday as the seventh-day Sabbath:

Because this change occurred so long ago, people today have forgotten the facts of history. It is impossible to find the Biblical Sabbath via a pagan calendar; therefore, Saturday cannot be the true Sabbath. Not knowing this, Saturday sabbatarians have assumed that Saturday is the Sabbath from which worship was removed. It is true that there are plenty of quotes from Catholic writers that refer to Saturday as "Sabbath"[3]

Sunday is founded, not of scripture, but on tradition, and is distinctly a Catholic institution. As there is no scripture for the transfer of the day of rest from the last to the first day of the week, *Protestants ought to keep their Sabbath on Saturday* and thus leave Catholics in full possession of Sunday. *Catholic Record,* September 17, 1893.[4]

Protestantism, in discarding the authority of the [Roman Catholic] Church, has no good reasons for its Sunday theory, and *ought logically to keep Saturday as the Sabbath.* John Gilmary Shea, *American Catholic Quarterly Review,* January 1883.[5]

Perhaps the boldest thing, the most revolutionary change the Church ever did, happened in the first century. *The holy day, the Sabbath, was changed from Saturday to Sunday.* The day of the

Lord was chosen, not from any direction noted in the Scriptures, but from the Church's sense of its own power...People who think that the Scriptures should be the sole authority, should logically become 7th Day Adventists, and *keep Saturday holy. St. Catherine Church Sentinel,* Algonac, Michigan, May 21, 1995.[6]

Is not every Christian obliged to sanctify Sunday and to abstain on that day from unnecessary servile work? Is not the observance of this law among the most prominent of our sacred duties? But you may read the Bible from Genesis to Revelation, and you will not find a single line authorizing the sanctification of Sunday. *The Scriptures enforce the religious observance of Saturday,* a day which we never sanctify. James Cardinal Gibbons, *The Faith of Our Fathers* (1917 edition), p. 72–73 (16th Edition, p. 111; 88th Edition, p. 89).[7]

Seventh-day Adventists have long used such quotes as admissions by the Catholic church that man changed the true Sabbath from Saturday to Sunday. However, Adventist doctrine has never been based on these writings. They have just been used as historical documentation. The Vornholts say that these Catholic writers are wrong because they are totally ignorant of accurate history. However, they say there is one Catholic scholar who knows the truth!

The facts of history having been forgotten by most people, many Catholic writers have used planetary week terminology (i.e., "Saturday"), which could be considered deceptive. It is also likely that many of the Catholic writers themselves were unaware of the full history behind the modern week. *However, Catholic scholars themselves have always known the truth.* As conservative Catholic scholar and apologist Patrick Madrid stated:[8]

[The] calendar that we follow, including Seventh-day Adventists, is not only a calendar that was devised by the Catholic Church, but also it is a calendar that's based upon the solar year, not the lunar year. And the Jewish calendar that was observed in the time of Christ . . . follows a lunar calendar, which is several days short of the solar year. So the great irony is that even the Seventh-day Adventists themselves are not worshiping on exactly the same Sabbath day as the Jews of the time of Christ. (quoted from Patrick Madrid on "Open Line," EWTN, Global Catholic Radio Network, January 5, 2006)[9]

Though the Vornholts discredit all of the Catholic quotes on everything on the topic of Sabbath/Sunday which do not agree with their theory, they believe that this one Catholic voice, Patrick Madrid, knows the truth about the calendar and the Sabbath because it supports the Lunar Sabbath. Making a Catholic scholar the "defender of truth" with the authority to define what is truth about one of the pillars of the Seventh-day Adventist faith, in direct opposition to the Spirit of Prophecy, raises a red flag.

And who is Patrick Madrid, whose word can be believed more than the last day prophet of the Lord? If you look at the website of Patrick Madrid[10] and read his biography, survey the classes and debates he offers, and note the glowing endorsements from the Vatican, you will realize that he is diametrically opposed to nearly everything Seventh-day Adventists hold as truth. It is obvious he also does not understand the separation of the Sabbath from the feasts and is not a reliable source for truth.

UNIVERSAL JEWISH ENCYCLOPEDIA

Another interesting quote from *History of a Lie* comes from the *Universal Jewish Encyclopedia* which clearly supports the Lunar Sabbath theory:

> The New Moon is still, and the Sabbath originally was, dependent upon the lunar cycle . . . Originally, the New Moon was celebrated in the same way as the Sabbath; gradually it became less important while the Sabbath became more and more a day of religion and humanity, of religious meditation and instruction, of peace and delight of the soul. "Holidays," *Universal Jewish Encyclopedia,* p. 410[11]

Nazarene Yisraelite Rabbi Tom (Mordecai) Mitchell (a Jewish scholar) has researched the Lunar Sabbath issue from the perspective of a Jew and uses Jewish historical records. He comments on the above quotation. He believes the Universal Jewish Encyclopedia has some serious credibility problems and he has some questions about the validity of this article.

> Attribution. Who wrote this article? The author's name is missing and that should be a "red flag" to readers. What are the author's qualifications and background? Is he (or she) an "expert" in the field of Ancient Near East history? These questions are left unanswered.

> Why is a Lunar Sabbath not addressed in the well-known "Jewish Encyclopedia," or in such recognized Jewish writings as the Talmud or Mishna?

> The author(s) of this article, whoever he, she or they might be, offer not one shred of historical evidence to document their claim. More importantly, not one shred of Scriptural evidence

is offered. The *Universal Jewish Encyclopedia* was in print from 1939 to 1944. The work never gained any acceptance among mainstream Judaism.[12]

While we cannot substantiate Rabbi Tom Mitchell's allegations against the *Universal Jewish Encyclopedia*, it does raise questions about its validity. If there were numerous respected Jewish encyclopedias, along with Jewish historians, that substantiated what this one encyclopedia says, it could be taken as more authoritative—but it stands as a lonely voice in support of the Lunar Sabbath theory.

A MODERN THEOLOGIAN

Pastor Smith[13] is a Seventh-day Adventist minister, and a mutual friend of mine and the Vornholts. Laura Lee Vornholt-Jones discussed the Lunar Sabbath theory with him and also sent him the manuscript for *The Great Calendar Controversy* and requested he give her feedback about it. He has concerns about the Lunar Sabbath theory as a whole, but he wrote an eleven page document in reply focusing specifically on the issues in the chapter regarding Daniel's prophecies. During my email interactions with Laura Lee, she made the following comments:

> One pastor, a friend(?), before the mailing went out [the mailing of *The Great Calendar Controversy* to numerous pastors and conference officials], objected to the chapter on Daniel. He accused us of deliberately using a wrong word in the translation of Daniel 8:11 to give a false and deceptive support to our argument... *(Incidentally, this was the same conservative SDA*

> *pastor that told me that I was correct: the Sabbath, when calculated by the Biblical calendar will fall differently, BUT all God requires is that we worship by whatever calendar society uses.)*[14]

Later, when her new book *History of a Lie* came out it said:

> Some modern theologians acknowledge, "Yes, when the seventh-day Sabbath is calculated by the Biblical calendar, it will fall differently; but all God requires of us is to keep the seventh-day Sabbath by whatever calendar society uses." Such a belief reveals a tragic lack of knowledge of the issues at stake.[15]

Because I knew Pastor Smith had been studying the Lunar Sabbath concept and had communicated with the Vornholts in regards to their beliefs, I asked him for any information he might have about it. He sent me the eleven page document of his study on the issues in Daniel. I realized immediately that he must be the "Modern Theologian" quoted in *History of a Lie.*" I could not imagine him making a statement like that, so I asked him about it. Here is his response:

> Yes, I am the pastor she is referring to. I do not believe in my document to her that I deliberately accused of her using wrong Hebrew words. I tried to give her and her mother the benefit of the doubt, and encouraged them to make corrections before printing the book.... I tried to leave things open for the possibility of an error, and at the same time clearly show that it would be dangerous to change the Word of God.

But what about the quote she made in her book? Did he say that?

I do not consider myself to be a modern theologian, but by God's grace try to be a Bible-based Pastor. I have tried to let them know that I am their friend.... In terms of their quote on page 18, I do not ever recall saying something like that. I have reviewed my e-mail communication with her, and could find nothing like that. As I have read this quote, I'm not even sure I know what it means.... At best, she may be tweaking something said in discussions in her living room a few years ago, at worst she is just drumming a particular straw man argument so she can easily knock it over. But I do not ever recall giving this particular quote.

Having an opportunity to go directly to the source of a quotation to discuss the meaning of what they are quoted as saying is unusual. In this case, it helped me to know without a doubt that the source was used in a questionable way.

WHAT'S LEFT?

In reviewing the structural support for the Lunar Sabbath theory, what remains seems weak. Whether intentional or unintentional, if research sources are questionable and the meanings of sources are twisted, the conclusions would also be questionable.

We must be very careful to explore the sources and compare them with the Bible. Are the meanings of words in harmony with Scripture or are they twisted to represent a false idea? We should not decide to believe in any new idea without careful study. And it doesn't take a theologian to learn what is right. God promises wisdom to anyone who desires to know the truth and surrenders to His Holy Spirit.

1. Vornholt, eLaine and Vornholt-Jones, Laura Lee. *History of a Lie* (Colbert, WA: 4 Angels Publications), p. 52, emphasis supplied.p. 30.

2. White, Ellen G. *The Great Controversy,* p. 447, emphasis supplied.

3. Vornholt, loc. cit., p. 35.

4. Ibid, emphasis supplied.

5. Ibid, emphasis supplied.

6. Ibid, emphasis supplied.

7. Ibid, emphasis supplied.

8. Vornholt, loc. cit., p. 36, emphasis supplied.

9. Ibid.

10. Patrickmadrid.com

11. Vornholt, loc. cit., p. 28.

12. Mitchell, Tom (Mordecai). "Lunar Sabbath: New Light or Sheer Lunacy?" see bnaiyeshurun.com/shee?lunacy.html

13. Not his real name.

14. Private email, emphasis supplied.

15. Vornholt, loc. cit., p. 18.

CHAPTER 14

THE SPIRIT
OF PROPHECY

USING DIVINE REVELATION—
ELLEN G. WHITE

The Bible provides several tests to distinguish God's true prophets. Seventh-day Adventists have put Ellen White through each of these tests, and besides having been a beautiful Christian person throughout her life, all the tests indicate that she was truly an instrument of God.

Ellen White experienced many heavenly visions in her 89 years. Many contained point by point details of our earth's history—from Lucifer's rebellion in heaven, Adam and Eve's sinless life in the garden, the Hebrew children struggling with sin, Christ's death on the cross, the unifying of the Adventist church's doctrines, to Christ coming again in the clouds and living in Heaven with Him. She saw and experienced much of it for herself. It was laid out before her in living images. Through vision she was an eyewitness to many events.

She stated, "As the Spirit of God has opened to my mind

the great truths of His word, and the scenes of the past and the future, I have been bidden to make known to others that which has thus been revealed—to trace the history of the controversy in past ages, and especially so to present it as to shed a light on the fast-approaching struggle of the future."[1]

Ellen White was human and had human traits and weaknesses, but she was an instrument for God. She used the inspiration from God in different ways: 1) sometimes dictating what God spoke to her, 2) writing down things shown her in her own descriptive words, or 3) finding inspired thoughts in her research of other writers to convey what God had revealed to her. This is the same way the Bible was inspired, "…for prophecy never came by the will of man, but holy men of God spoke as they were moved by the Holy Spirit."[2]

While the Lunar Sabbath authors say they have utmost faith in the Spirit of Prophecy and claim they do not intend to discredit Ellen White, they disagree with her many plain statements throughout their books, articles, and website. Here are some brief examples of contradictions:

Ellen White	Lunar Sabbath Authors
Affirms the Sabbath falling on the seventh day, Saturday.	Claim Ellen White was ignorant of the final day truth in her time.
Says that God preserved the weekly cycle since Creation to the present.	Say that the weekly cycle is a pagan institution.

States clearly that Jesus died on Friday and was in the tomb by sunset when the Sabbath arrived.	Say Jesus died on what we know as Wednesday.
Repeatedly talks about the Sabbath beginning at sundown.	Claim that Sabbath begins at sunrise.
Makes very clear statements about Sunday being the idol Sabbath.	State that Saturday is more the idolatrous Sabbath than Sunday.
Claims that we must keep the Sabbath on Saturday in order to receive the Seal of God in the final days.	Deny Saturday is the day of the true Sabbath and claim that keeping it is a deception of Satan.
Encourages the spread of the seventh-day Sabbath (on Saturday) throughout the world.	Claim that the Lunar Sabbath and not the "Saturday" seventh-day Sabbath should be spread abroad.
Said plainly that Sunday is a specific day of worship that will result in people having the mark of the beast.	Assert that end-time Sunday laws are actually just calendar changes throwing off the week as we know it.

If the authors' claims are true, these contradictions must mean that Ellen White was more than just ignorant of truth and unknowingly teaching error, especially when she claims Jesus Christ Himself showed her the true Sabbath.

How could God, in giving Ellen White explicit and clear visions in detail about the Sabbath and the time of the end, fail to give her such critical information about the final test in earth's history? How could He actually give her wrong messages to share with the world? How could He allow His last day prophet to teach a pagan, idolatrous deception that would cause His remnant church, His beloved bride, to receive the mark of the beast if they followed her plain teachings?

ELLEN WHITE AND SATURDAY

In another Lunar Sabbatarian's personal e-mail to me, the author claimed that Ellen White never really said that Saturday was the true Sabbath day. This must be ignorance on this author's part for, as one of the founders of the Seventh-day Adventist church which has kept Saturday as the Sabbath since its inception, Ellen White believed the day known as Saturday to be the true seventh-day Sabbath. She made many clear statements that Saturday is the Sabbath. Here are just a few:

> Many declared that the enterprise could not be maintained if it *closed its doors on Saturday. But since the Sabbath closing, a special blessing has manifestly rested upon the work.*[3]

> The temptation will come. *If you keep the Sabbath, the very day the fourth commandment has specified,* you shall have to give up this source of gain. *You shall have to close your business on Saturday,* the busiest and most profitable day in the week.[4]

A neighbor came in during one evening. During the course of the conversation this woman asked Ellen White whether she would explain to her about the Sabbath. She describes what then took place:

> "I began by reading a text in the first of Genesis. Then I read the fourth commandment. When I had read this, they said, 'Yes, but Sunday is the seventh day.' I explained to them that Sunday is the first day, and that *the day called Saturday by the world is*

the seventh day. Then I read the last six verses of the thirty-first chapter of Exodus, where the Sabbath is clearly specified as the sign between God and His people."[5]

She also had numerous diary entries throughout her lifetime that defined Saturday as the Sabbath, such as this one:

Saturday, January 11, 1873: We rested well last night. This Sabbath morning opens cloudy.[6]

NEW LIGHT

Lunar Sabbatarians claim their view is "new light" for these last days. To change from the belief that Saturday is the seventh day according to the commandment, as taught by the Seventh-day Adventist church and Ellen White, to a totally different method would definitely take some strong new light on the subject.

The Great Calendar Controversy says that Seventh-day Adventists want a plain "thus saith the Lord" or clear Ellen White quotes before we'll accept new light and that we demand a clear, single statement rather than using the process of digging for truth as for hidden treasure.[7]

It is true that doctrinal truth must be searched out from various places of the Bible. But when it comes to beliefs about issues as important as the true Sabbath of the Ten Commandments and who receives the mark of the beast, there had better be clear evidence to support it.

Ellen White did not give any new light in regards to

changing the method of determining the Sabbath day. The only quotations from the Spirit of Prophecy that the Lunar Sabbatarians use to support their ideas are some that say we will receive and understand new light before the Lord comes.

There are many statements from the Spirit of Prophecy which show that while there is much light to receive, the new light will never contradict the foundational truths God has led us to know. Ellen White warned us about new light changing the truth. Here is just a small sample of those statements:

> *We are not to receive the words of those who come with a message that contradicts the special points of our faith.* They gather together a mass of Scripture, and pile it as proof around their asserted theories. This has been done over and over again during the past fifty years. And while the Scriptures are God's word, and are to be respected, the application of them, *if such application moves one pillar from the foundation that God has sustained these fifty years, it is a great mistake.*[8]

New light must be approached with a prayerful and open mind, holding it up to Scripture and the Spirit of Prophecy. If the new light conflicts with the foundational doctrines of the Seventh-day Adventist faith, which have been proven in scripture and through the clear revelation of the Holy Spirit, it is to be rejected as false light. New and deeper understandings of truth will come, but new light cannot be true if it rejects or contradicts the truths God gave before.

MODERN LOGIC VS. DIVINE REVELATION

An interesting statement from *The Great Calendar Controversy* says, "...the cycle of weeks never was intended to be continuous as the lunar months interrupted it. The church has to deal with this truth. It cannot be shrugged off with, 'Well, if the Bible and Ellen White don't agree with the U.S. Naval Observatory, you know which one is wrong—it's the U.S. Naval Observatory!' It is *not* wrong."[9]

What they are saying is that the U.S. Naval Observatory's (USNO) calculations cannot be wrong when it supposedly supports an aspect of their theory which directly conflicts with the plain word of the Spirit of Prophecy. But is it safe to discover truth using a human institution as a greater authority than Divine inspiration?

If we used that logic, we should believe in Evolution, because renowned worldly scientific organizations say it is true. Millions of Christians have been deceived into believing in Evolution because science has seemed to "prove" it is correct. Others have thrown out the Bible as a hoax because "scientific evidence" has shown that the miracles and teachings in God's Word cannot be proven by human reasoning.

Perhaps the USNO and the Bible and Spirit of Prophecy are all correct and it is our understanding of what they are each saying that is the problem. When we don't understand something, isn't it better to take clear statements from God's Word and the Spirit of Prophecy as the basis of truth—

and then seek to see how evidence and logic actually can support God's revelations?

There are some things on earth which we will never fully understand, but we must take God at His Word and live by faith until that day when we are shown how and why things happened. Many times, especially in the field of archeology, "facts" that embarrassed Christians have later been shown to confirm what God said.

It is better to trust in the Lord than to put confidence in man.[10]

1. White, Ellen G. *The Great Controversy,* p. xi.

2. 2 Peter 1:21.

3. White, Ellen G. *Review & Herald,* (February 19, 1901) par. 6, emphasis supplied.

4. White, Ellen G. *Manuscript Releases,* Vol. 17, p. 79, emphasis supplied.

5. White, Arthur. *Ellen G. White:* Vol. 5, p. 330, emphasis supplied.

6. White, Ellen G. *Manuscript Releases,* Vol. 8, p. 448, emphasis supplied.

7. Vornholt, eLaine and Vornholt-Jones, Laura Lee. *The Great Calendar Controversy* (Colbert, WA: 4 Angels Publications), p. 1.

8. White, Ellen G. *Counsels to Writers and Editors,* p. 32, emphasis supplied.

9. Vornholt, loc. cit., p. 37, emphasis supplied.

10. Psalm 118:8.

CHAPTER 15

DON'T MAKE A MISTAKE

THE FINAL TEST TOO OBVIOUS?

Seventh-day Adventists believe Scripture and the Spirit of Prophecy teach that there will be a test over the true Sabbath at the end of time. Legal enforcement of Sunday as the day to rest and worship, known as the Sunday Law, will reveal those who are willing to be faithful to God in keeping the true Sabbath on pain of death.

The Great Calendar Controversy declares the Sunday law at the end of time is not about the world designating a false day in place of the true, but rather an issue of a calendar change disguised to deceive Seventh-day Adventists. "Not recognizing that the change of calendar law is the Sunday law, many will preach that we need to go along with it."[1]

According to their book, a literal Sunday law is too obvious of a test because Seventh-day Adventists know about it already. "What kind of a test is that?" the authors ask, "since everyone already knows about it?" Therefore, they say the final test will be a secretive change in order to slip it past our notice and only those who learn of the secret will avoid the mark of the beast.

> Think about it. Satan's main target is the Seventh-day Adventist church. Everyone knows about Sunday closing laws and all have assumed that is the form the Sunday law will take. But if you were Satan, and your #1 enemy was expecting that plan of attack, would you not try and slip it past without their notice?[2]

Jesus came to save His people from Satan. Throughout the Bible He always gave clear warnings and instructions to His people before each major test and trial they faced.

In the story of Adam and Eve, God gave a direct command not to eat of the Tree of Knowledge of Good and Evil. He even stated what the consequences were going to be—they would die. Could there be any simpler test given to prove loyalty to God? All they had to do was avoid the tree. The problem was that Eve allowed the devil to deceive her and she choose not to trust God. The test was simple and obvious but Eve still failed because "self" took over. This is actually the choice we make in all tests, whether we choose to surrender to our evil "flesh" or to God, whether we choose to trust self or trust God.

God's warning regarding the flood was very clear. Noah preached for 120 years, begging the people to follow God and avoid the destruction coming upon the world. Yet no one, except Noah and his family, entered the ark. The test was clear and well defined; just walk up the gang plank and into the ark. Everyone knew exactly how that could be done and the results if they didn't, but the outcome of that test was devastating.

Another example concerned Daniel's friends, the three Hebrew boys. They, as well as the other Jewish captives, knew the king was going to order all who came to Dura to bow down and worship his golden idol on the given day. The punishment for not bowing was death—simple, obvious. God had given the command to His people that no one was to bow down and worship any god other than Him— also a clear command and obvious to all the Hebrews. But when the test came, the three Hebrew boys were the only ones who chose to follow God. Why? Because the other Hebrews did not have a strong faith in God. Their selfish natures caused them to go along with the crowd due to pride, peer pressure, and/or fear of death.

A clear picture of what the last days might be like for observers of the true Sabbath is exemplified in the dark ages. Those who chose to remain faithful to God's Word faced horrific torture, stabbings, persecution, dark dungeons, confiscation of property, displacement, starvation, and martyrdom. These Christians loved God for the deep, satisfying peace He put in their lives and they were willing to follow His every command to the death. But how many Christians failed this clear test of trusting in God because they were not willing to go through what it required of them?

Are we willing to give up everything and endure hardships to wholly trust in God? Ellen White says that only those who learn to endure hardships will make it to the end.

Doesn't this sound like a test? We all have the same choice every day. Are we going to let inconvenience and difficulties keep us from being loyal to God? Or will we resist by doing things on our own?

In the coming Sunday law, again the test is obvious. God commanded we are to worship only on the seventh-day Sabbath because it shows our loyalty to Him. If we don't keep His sanctified Sabbath we receive the mark of the beast and are doomed to eternal loss. It may seem like a simple test, but many will fail just like the majority of the Hebrews at Dura who wanted to avoid the hardships, persecution, and death that would come from following God's command.

THE FINAL TEST A SECRET?

Why should the final test in earth's history be secretive and extremely difficult to uncover? It shouldn't. The final test involves the whole world, not just Seventh-day Adventists, and the coming Sunday law is not obvious to most of the world. God opened up the truth and made it plain as to what the test in the time of trouble would be. It is not about calendar change, for this is not what He revealed. God has no reason to keep the details of the test from us. He desires to save as many as He can.

> Surely, the Lord God does nothing, unless He reveals His secret to His servants the prophets.[3]

The good news is that God does not expect us to go through this test alone. He gives us plenty of information to make a smart choice.

> *There are many in the churches of our country who have never, even in this land of light and knowledge, had an opportunity to hear the special truths for this time.* The obligation of the fourth commandment has never been set before them in its true light. Jesus reads every heart, and tries every motive. The decree is not to be urged upon the people blindly. *Every one is to have sufficient light to make his decision intelligently.* The Sabbath will be the great test of loyalty; for it is the point of truth especially controverted.[4]

CHOOSING THE RIGHT PATH

The "Saturday" Sabbath and the Lunar Sabbath cannot both be correct. All the arguments seem to boil down to whether God tied the Sabbath to the same method as calculating the feasts by the moon, or if He set up a weekly cycle at Creation for the Sabbath and preserved it to our day. I find no conclusive evidence in scripture pointing to the Sabbath being tied to the moon. What Lunar Sabbatarians have given as facts are insufficient, compared to plain statements by God's Word, the Spirit of Prophecy, and history in support of a "Saturday" Sabbath.

Why is this test so important anyway? Why should we be concerned about the right day? Because God made it clear in Revelation that the seventh-day Sabbath issue is going to be our greatest test in the final days before Jesus' second coming—a test of our loyalty to Him. Those who reject the truth of the Sabbath will receive the mark of the beast. When a person receives this mark, their doom is sealed forever. They will never experience the love and joy of heaven and the perfect peace and trust of those around.

> God has given men the Sabbath as a sign between Him and them, as a test of their loyalty. Those who, after the light regarding God's law comes to them, continue to disobey and exalt human laws above the law of God in the great crisis before us will receive the mark of the beast.[5]

One day I visited with a father who told me about his daughter who deeply promoted the Lunar Sabbath. She pled that he would accept the "truth" because she didn't want to see him lost at the end of the world. Of course, this father has the same heart-wrenching feelings for his daughter's salvation. Both feel the power of conviction, but one is based on the Word of God and the other is not.

> There is a way that seems right to a man, but its end is the way of death.[6]

There lies ahead of us a junction of two paths in regards to determining the Sabbath. One path is true and leads to the Kingdom of Heaven, while the other is a deceptive path leading to eternal darkness. It is crucial that we choose the path of truth, trusting in the plain word of God, rather than theories. Don't make a mistake! Study this out for yourself!

I pray that you will have a solid belief in the true Sabbath of the Lord. Having a sure faith in knowing that you understand the truth of the Sabbath will bring peace as well as confidence in following God's will when standing for His truth in the last days.

1. Vornholt, eLaine and Vornholt-Jones, Laura Lee. *The Great Calendar Controversy* (Colbert, WA: 4 Angels Publications), p. 63.
2. Vornholt, loc. cit., p. 51.
3. Amos 3:7.
4. White, Ellen G. *The Spirit of Prophecy,* Vol. 4, p. 422, emphasis supplied.
5. White, Ellen G. *Evangelism,* p. 235.
6. Proverbs 16:25.

Made in the USA
Middletown, DE
27 August 2023

37261124R00092